Policing Race and Place in Indian Country

Critical Perspectives on Crime and Inequality

Series Editor
Walter S. DeKeseredy, University of Ontario Institute of Technology

Advisory Board
Shahid Alvi, University of Ontario Institute of Technology
Meda Chesney-Lind, University of Hawaii at Manoa
Mark Israel, Flinders University of South Australia
Barbara Perry, University of Ontario Institute of Technology
Claire Renzetti, Saint Joseph's University
Martin Schwartz, Ohio University

Critical Perspectives on Crime and Inequality presents cutting edge work informed by these schools of thought: feminism, peacemaking criminology, left realism, Marxism, cultural criminology, and postmodernism. In an age of instrumental reason and increasing state control, the need for critical and independent analysis of power and social arrangements has never been more acute. Books published in this series will be monographs for scholars and researchers, as well as texts for course use.

Titles in Series:

The Politics of Organized Crime and the Organized Crime of Politics, by Alfredo Schulte-Bockholt

Advancing Critical Criminology: Theory and Application, edited by Walter S. DeKeseredy and Barbara Perry

Symbolic Gestures and the Generation of Global Social Control, by Dawn Rothe and Christopher W. Mullins

Charting Women's Journeys, by Judith Grant

Criminal to Critic, by James E. Palombo with Randall G. Shelden

Policing Race and Place in Indian Country: Over- and Underenforcement, by Barbara Perry

Policing Race and Place in Indian Country

Over- and Underenforcement

BARBARA PERRY

LEXINGTON BOOKS

A division of
ROWMAN & LITTLEFIELD PUBLISHERS, INC.
Lanham • Boulder • New York • Toronto • Plymouth, UK

LEXINGTON BOOKS

A division of Rowman & Littlefield Publishers, Inc.
A wholly owned subsidiary of The Rowman & Littlefield Publishing Group, Inc.
4501 Forbes Boulevard, Suite 200
Lanham, MD 20706

Estover Road
Plymouth PL6 7PY
United Kingdom

Copyright © 2009 by Lexington Books

British Library Cataloguing in Publication Information Available

Library of Congress Cataloging-in-Publication Data

Perry, Barbara, 1962-
    Policing race and place in Indian country : over- and underenforcement / Barbara
Perry.
        p. cm. -- (Critical perspectives on crime and inequality)
    Includes bibliographical references and index.
    ISBN-13: 978-0-7391-1613-5 (cloth : alk. paper)
    ISBN-10: 0-7391-1613-4 (cloth : alk. paper)
    ISBN-13: 978-0-7391-3217-3 (electronic : alk. paper)
    ISBN-10: 0-7391-3217-2 (electronic : alk. paper)
  1. Indians of North America--Crimes against. 2. Indian reservation
police--United States. 3. Law enforcement--United States. I. Title.
    E98.C87P44 2009
    323.1197--dc22   2008035540

Printed in the United States of America

⊖™ The paper used in this publication meets the minimum requirements of American
National Standard for Information Sciences—Permanence of Paper for Printed Library
Materials, ANSI/NISO Z39.48–1992.

To First Nations people everywhere

Contents

Figures ix
Tables xi
Acknowledgements xiii

1 Introduction: Missing Pieces 1

2 Racialized Policing 13

3 Colonial Policing and Beyond 33

4 Over-policing Native American Communities 47

5 Under-policing Native American Communities 61

6 Impacts of Disparate Policing 77

7 Policing Differently? 91

Bibliography 105
Index 115
About the Author 117

Figures

Figure 1.1 Number of violent victimizations, by race   4

Figure 1.2 American Indians as percent of
     all violent offenders entering Federal Prisons,
     1994-2001   5

Tables

Table 1.1 Murders of American Indians,
     as a percent of all American Indians
     and of all murder victims, by State, 1976-1999   5

Table 1.2 Arrests by Alcohol Violations, Race and Age, 2001   5

Table 2.1 National Estimate of Racial Profiling   25

Table 3.1 Eras of Policing in Indian Country   35

Table 3.2 State-by-State Overview of PL280   43

Table 3.3 Types of Indian Police Departments
     and Their Characteristics   44

Table 5.1 Sample Comparisons of
     UCR Hate Crime Data to Those Collected
     by Anti-Violence Organizations   66

Table 5.2. The Hate Crime Reporting Process   67

Table 6.1. Native American Incarceration Rate by State   79

Acknowledgements

My first debt of gratitude unquestionably goes to all of those people who gave so freely of their time and wisdom during the interviews. This work would not have been possible without their kindness. I hope it goes some way to bringing to light their experiences, and consequently, some change.

I next thank the wonderful colleagues, especially at Northern Arizona University and the University of Ontario Institute of Technology, who have inspired me and who have also shared their own brand of wisdom over the years: Dr. Alex Alvarez; Dr. Shahid Alvi; Dr. Walter DeKeseredy; Dr. Larry Gould; Dr. Ray Michalowski; and Dr. Marianne Nielsen.

I am also deeply appreciative of the support offered by Northern Arizona University during my eight years there. The initial pilot study on which this work is based was made possible by a grant from the University's Intramural Summer Grants Program. The University also supported my sabbatical, during which I conducted the interviews in Montana, Wisconsin, and Minnesota. This latter leg of the project was funded by a United States Department of Agriculture Grant (Rural Development Initiative).

While in the field, I was very fortunate to hire three outstanding Research Assistants: Paulita Smith (Navajo, Arizona); Matthew Ryan (Ojibwe, Wisconsin); and Ryan Kennedy (Black Foot, Montana). All three did a remarkable job helping me to access participants, understand the communities, and conduct the interviews. Thanks to all of you. I hope the work was as meaningful to you as it was to me. And I hope that it somehow proves to be of some strategic value as you pursue related employment.

Of course, no academic lives in a vacuum. Few of us could survive emotionally or intellectually without a circle that nurtures them. For me, this has been constituted by my family, and especially by my parents, Keith and Joanne Perry, who continue to spoil me even now! And the heart of my circle, as always, is my husband Michael Groff. Inexplicably, he is still here and still my biggest fan.

Chapter 1
Introduction: Missing Pieces

It is puzzling that a 2001 NIJ Research Report entitled *Policing on American Indian Reservations* makes no more than passing reference to the uneasy relationship between Aboriginal peoples and law enforcement agencies (Wakeling, Jorgensen, Michaelson, and Begay, 2001). This is ironic in light of the fact that the report tends to focus on an initiative—tribal policing—intended to ameliorate exactly that problem. This oversight flies in the face of the historical legacy of racism that permeates the policing of Indian Country. However, it is consistent the ongoing scholarly neglect of systemic discrimination experienced by Native Americans within the context of the criminal justice system. While attention to racism within policing, specifically, has increased in recent years, the emphasis has largely been on the experiences of African Americans and Latinos, with very little consideration of the plight of Native Americans.

This book seeks to address this important void, by exploring the ways in which Native American communities—especially those in and around reservations—are both over- and under-policed in ways that perpetuate both the criminalization and victimization of Native Americans as nations and as individuals. This argument is illustrated by drawing upon a series of interviews conducted with 278 Native Americans from seven states. While the interviews were primarily concerned with uncovering patterns of hate crime against Native Americans, dissatisfaction with police was a frequently raised issue. Consequently, the current work emerges from the common observations made by participants about the nature of law enforcement in their communities. It became readily apparent that police were perceived to be simultaneously under- and over-enforcing the law in American Indian communities. Participants reported activities ranging from willful blindness to Native American victimization at one extreme, to overt forms of police harassment and violence at the other end of the continuum.

The analysis is contextualized, first, with a brief discussion of the role of the state, generally, in the politics and policing of race, and of the historical relationship between the state and Native American communities. What emerges from this contextual introduction is the recognition that the patterns observed by the participants of the study are an extension of a lengthy history of systemic racism against Native Americans. This is the focus of the remainder of the book, in which it is argued that law enforcement perpetuates marginalization and disempowerment by simultaneously over- and under-policing Native American communities.

1

Exploring Native American Justice Issues

It is only in the last decade, perhaps less, that academics have begun to se-riously attend to Native American justice issues. While scholarly attention to black and even Hispanic subjugation at the hands of the criminal justice system has reached at least its late adolescence, parallel research on Native American victimization, offending and criminal justice processing is still in its infancy. Archambeault (2003), for instance, discovered from a sample of 285 articles in mainstream criminology and criminal justice journals and government publications (1995-2002) that only twenty-one focused exclu-sively on Native Americans, and only seven treated them on a par with other racialized groups. In fact, all but two of these were government reports. In contrast, over two-thirds completely neglected Native Americans—99% of the journal articles failed in this respect (Archambeault, 2003).

With a few outstanding exceptions (e.g., Nielsen and Silverman, 1996; Nielsen and Silverman, forthcoming; Ross and Gould, 2006), there is little scholarly work devoted to the specificity of the American Indian experience with respect to American criminal justice processes. Moreover, tracing the bibliographies of the limited scholarship is less than informative, as the works generally offer few leads toward more sophisticated analyses. No wonder, then, that it has proven exceptionally difficult to unearth literature specifically on policing Native American communities. This body of litera-ture is even more limited in quantity and quality. Even policing journals are largely silent on this issue. For example, from 2000 to 2007, *Police Practice and Research* featured only one article specifically addressing Aboriginal justice issues. A special edition in 2003 (Vol. 4, Ed. 4) was devoted to res-torative justice, but not exclusively (or even primarily) as practiced by Ab-original communities. Eileen Luna-Firebaugh is one of the few scholars to methodically examine law enforcement in Indian Country (see Luna-Firebaugh, 2007), but her emphasis tends to be on jurisdictional issues, ra-ther than on a critical analysis of the role of law enforcement in policing racialized boundaries.

Another dramatic limitation within the literature is that work that pro-fesses to explore racism in policing tends to focus primarily on African Americans. Given the relatively high concentration of blacks within the United States, this is perhaps not surprising. As noted, much less common are critical analyses of the ways in which Native Americans are policed. One must turn to Canadian and Australian literature for sophisticated work on the ways in which the policing of Aboriginal peoples are inextricably bound up with the legacy of colonization (e.g., Hylton, 2002; Neugebauer, 1999; Cunneen, 2001; Royal Commission on Deaths in Custody; Royal Commission on Aboriginal People, 1996). While American police were chasing down escaped slaves, Australian and Canadian officers were polic-ing the boundaries of the scattered reserves; while American police were celebrating lynchings, Canadian and Australian police were helping with the forced removal of First Nations and Aboriginal children from their homes.

Finally, the little literature that does deal with American Indian justice concerns tends toward decidedly atheoretical and uncritical approaches. The most heavily cited accounts, for example, are the NIJ report on *Policing on American Indian Reservations* (Wakeling et al., 2001), and Barker's (1998) *Policing in Indian Country*. None of these offer much in the way of criticism of the ways and means of policing American Indians. Nor do they even imply the ways in which both historical and contemporary police practices have been firmly embedded in ideologies of racism and colonialism. Rather, the authors of such work tend to be apologists for law enforcement, occasionally citing only bureaucratic problems which are deemed to be amenable to "quick fixes."

In short, what is absent in the two bodies of literature—that on Native American justice issues, and that on racism in policing—is an attempt to bring the two together. Since first contact, white authorities in the United States, as well as other similar colonial nations have sought to contain the "threat" posed by Aboriginal peoples through the full continuum of genocidal and ethnocidal practices: village massacres, forced marches, the willful introduction of deadly (to American Indians) disease, forced removal of children to boarding schools, and banning traditional rites and ceremonies (Stannard, 1992). The front line for such operations frequently included police authorities—or what substituted for police authorities. Consequently, for many Native Americans, police are inseparable from the broader white culture and white domination. They have become symbolic of the state and all it represents. In light of the fact that racism is embedded in both the dominant culture and the police subculture, Native Americans "undoubtedly expect trouble from the police" (Neugebauer, 1999: 248). And trouble they get, if my participants' experiences are in fact typical.

The paucity of research on Native American issues is more than simply perplexing. It is disturbing. Native Americans represent the most disproportionately over-represented population both in terms of victimization, and arrest and incarceration rates. The latter is not to suggest that Native Americans are more likely to be "criminal" than other racial or ethnic groups. Rather, it is to argue that they are disproportionately criminalized, a very different interpretation. Typically, this has been presented as and either/or dichotomy: either they commit more crimes than their white counterparts, or they are disparately treated by law enforcement and the courts. Yet this is too simplistic. Indeed, criminalization must not been seen as an incident attributable to the actions of one or the other, but as a process that takes into account historic and contemporary patterns of colonization and oppression, in concert with the machinations of the justice system. Chris Cunneen (2001: 25) calls for an analysis that takes into account diverse interconnected and mutually reinforcing conditions:

> The factors necessary to explain Aboriginal over-representation include particular offending patterns; the impact of policing; legal factors; judicial decision-making; environmental and locational factors; cultural difference; socioeconomic factors; marginalisation; resistance and the impact of colonization.

In short, to understand the criminalization of Native Americans, one must consider both sides of the equation: the criminogenic conditions in which many Native Americans live, and the nature of policing in Native American communities.

The 2004 BJS report entitled *American Indians and Crime* (Perry, 2004) paints a dismal portrait of Native American involvement in crime. They are much more likely to become victims of crime than members of any other racial group, experiencing crime at a rate of one in ten, or twice that of the general population (see figure 1.1). Also telling are the facts that they were more likely to be victims of inter-racial than intra-racial crime (Perry, 2004), and that they are very likely to be victimized by a stranger than someone they know crime than any other group. And, while their representation as victims of homicide—nationally—is proportionate to their representation in the population, this occludes regional differences. Indeed, in states where there is a relatively large concentration of Native Americans, they tend to over-represented as murder victims (see table 1.1).

Figure 1.1
Number of violent victimizations, by race

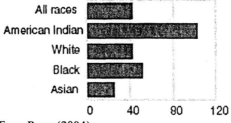

From Perry (2004)

Native Americans are also over-represented in arrest and corrections statistics. This is especially the case for DUI, public drunkenness, and liquor law violations. The fact that so many—nearly twice the proportion relative to the population (see table 1.1)—are arrested for alcohol related offenses testifies to the dysfunction that has been created by colonial processes that have left Native American communities impoverished and deculturated (Gould, 2006). It also raises questions about the extent to which Native Americans—especially in Indian Country—might be subject to greater visibility and scrutiny by law enforcement. Finally, they are consistently and dramatically over-represented as a proportion of offenders entering Federal prisons (see figure 1.2). Consequently, like African Americans, Native Americans are disproportionately likely to be under the control of the justice system.

Table 1.1

**Murders of American Indians, as a percent of all American Indians and of
all murder victims, by State, 1976-1999**

States with the largest number of American Indian murder victims	Number of murders of American Indians	Percent of — All murders of American Indians	Percent of — Total American Indian population	American Indians as a percent of — All murder victims	American Indians as a percent of — Total resident population
U.S. total	3,208	100.0%	100.0%	0.7%	0.9%
California	425	13.2	13.5	0.6	1.0
Oklahoma	374	11.7	11.0	6.3	7.9
Alaska	313	9.8	4.0	28.1	15.6
North Carolina	297	9.3	4.0	2.1	1.2
Arizona	269	8.4	10.3	3.9	5.0
Washington	204	6.4	3.8	4.0	1.6
New Mexico	192	6.0	7.0	7.5	9.5
Minnesota	183	5.7	2.2	7.0	1.1
New York	88	2.7	3.3	0.2	0.4
Oregon	75	2.3	1.8	2.5	1.3
All other States	788	24.5	39.0	0.2	0.4

From Perry (2004)

Figure 1.2

American Indians as percent of all violent offenders entering Federal Prisons, 1994-2001

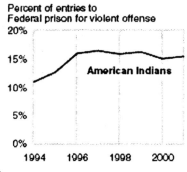

Percent of entries to
Federal prison for violent offense

From Perry (2004)

Table 1.2

Arrests by Alcohol Violations, Race and Age, 2001

	All Races	American Indian
Total alcohol violations	623	1,240
Driving under the influence	332	479
Liquor laws	143	405
Drunkenness	148	356

From Perry (2004)

The Project

This analysis is largely informed by a larger project which represents the first large scale empirical exploration of hate crime against American Indians. Three related projects were conducted: a 1999 pilot study undertaken in the Four Corners region (funded by the Office of Intramural Grants at NAU); a campus hate crime survey of Native American students at NAU; and a 2002/2003 study in the Great Lakes, and the northern plains region (funded by USDA). In total, interviews or surveys were conducted with 278 Native Americans from seven states (Arizona, Colorado, Minnesota, Montana, New Mexico, Utah, and Wisconsin), representing eight American Indian nations (Apache, Navajo, Hopi, Ojibwe, Crow, Blackfeet, Salish/Kootenai, and Northern Cheyenne), and representing more than a dozen reservations. More than half (146) of the participants were women; participants ranged in age from sixteen to eighty-two.

During visits to American Indian reservations and nearby border towns, a series of semi-structured interviews canvassing Native American experiences of hate crime were conducted. There is widespread consensus among scholars who work with Native American communities that face to face interviews must be the primary means of soliciting insights from Indigenous Peoples (Grenier, 1998; Guyette, 1983). For the most part, these communities are grounded in an oral tradition. Interviews, therefore, allow information to be gathered in a narrative, story-telling mode that is familiar and comfortable to participants. Moreover, the utility of surveys is limited, first by the suspicion with which many Native American participants regard the written word. As Marianne Nielsen (2000: 11) has expressed it, written surveys "are far too reminiscent of broken treaties." On the basis of her extensive research among Indigenous Peoples in Canada, the United States, New Zealand and Australia, Nielsen concludes that

> Many Indigenous cultures emphasize oral tradition, and have little regard for written documents. This can manifest itself in a number of ways. The author has been told by older people, for example, that it is disrespectful to take notes during an interview. It may also mean that people will simply refuse to fill out the questionnaire, thereby biasing the non-response rate by excluding people with more traditional values. Because of its highly structured nature, a survey design may also lose the nuances of the data, or miss getting an answer, altogether (Nielsen, 2000: 10).

Practically, the use of surveys is also restricted by the fact that many Native Americans on reservations—particularly elders—have little to no proficiency in reading or writing English. The interview process, then, ensured the most extensively nuanced responses possible. And, in all likelihood, such an approach maximized participants' willingness to share their stories.

It is also important to note that, in each region, an American Indian Research Assistant was hired. She or he assisted in the development and conduct of a culturally sensitive interview. In addition, they helped to ensure that the key concepts could be translated into the Native languages. The presence of Native American Research Assistants, typically from the areas in question, undoubtedly helped to bridge the cultural distance between the Native American participants and the non-Native researcher. In addition to the on-site interviews, there was also a survey of Native American students at NAU, which tapped their experiences of racial violence and discrimination on campus.[1]

Given the wide dispersal of what might be called "Indian Country," conducting all of the interviews in the homes of subjects was not viable. The travel costs and time required were prohibitive. In addition, there exists no accurate census of Native Americans that could have been consulted to create a random sample. Consequently, a combination of convenience and snowball sampling was employed. The Principal Investigator and Research Assistants spent seven to ten days in each state. Volunteers were solicited in a number of public locales, ranging from Indian Centers, to government offices, to public libraries. Others were arranged or suggested by participants and other contacts in the field. Many of these interviews were, in fact, conducted in the homes of participants. For the most part, then, subjects were in a relatively familiar and unthreatening setting (Grenier, 1998).

By its very nature, ethnoviolence is a controversial subject of inquiry. It forces consideration of individual trauma and suffering (physical and psychic), intergroup tensions and conflicts, and chinks in the armor of democracy and egalitarianism. This research faced additional barriers because of the nature of the population involved. Colleagues warned that there would have great difficulty in gaining access to the Native American community; and that Native American people would be unwilling, even afraid to talk openly about their experiences and perceptions of racial discrimination and violence. Fortunately, the opposite turned out to be true. In all but one of the sites, participants were genuinely eager to share their experiences of racial violence and discrimination. In one town, those approached consistently refused to participate. Typically, they would decline saying that it would be a waste of time. There appeared to be a widespread sense that whatever was said would have little impact on the lives of individuals or their communities. More typical, however, were those who gladly shared their perceptions and experiences. At one location, people were literally lined up out the door of the office used to conduct interviews. Especially rewarding were those interviews in which participants expressed gratitude for the efforts to uncover what seemed to them to be the invisible and hidden practices of violence. These expressed the following sentiment: "I'm glad you're here. I think this is really important work that no one has wanted to do before. Your questions are welcome here; the answers, I hope the answers will help us here and other Indian tribes too" (Male, New Mexico).

The interviews addressed the dynamics of violent and non-violent victimization. Consequently, they reflected the following concepts: hate crime (e.g., verbal insults, harassment, physical violence, dynamics, location); oppression/discrimination (e.g., chronic unemployment); reporting of ethnoviolence; and recommendations for responding to hate crime. Moreover, special attention was paid to the extent to which violence was perceived to be motivated by recent or current activism on the part of local Native American communities. Additionally, a great deal of time in these interviews was devoted to the question of policies and practices that might enhance relationships between communities, and thus drive down the incidence of hate crime.

The observations about law enforcement emerged out of conversations about reporting practices and about participants' perceptions of the relationship between Native Americans and the criminal justice system. I initially included these questions only because they are "standard" in most victim research on hate crime. I could not have anticipated how emphatic participants would be in their indictment of police as enablers, if not participants in the racial harassment and violence directed toward Native Americans. Quite unexpectedly, this became a powerful theme across interviews and across venues. It quickly became apparent to me that this was an untapped area of exploration, and therefore worthy of concentrated attention.

Before proceeding, the reader should be aware of the patterns of racist violence that emerged in the interviews. The majority of participants had either themselves been victims, or knew of someone close to them who had been victims, of some form of hate crime—ranging from verbal harassment to pushing and shoving to brutal assaults with knives and lighter fluid. By far the most common incidents were various types of name calling and verbal harassment on the street and in commercial establishments, such as the following example:

> I think Gallup is the same way, I think Gallup is, is uh worse. Uh, Gallup is worse, because you can feel the stares, and me, myself, I don't take these things laying down. If I see someone looking at me that, that I know is thinking, what are you doing with this Anglo, I speak right away 'What the hell you looking at boy, you damn right I'm an Indian.' You know, I'm not going to take this stand, sitting down anymore, cause I, I've had incidences where I've been called a "damn prairie nigger," "chief," "blanket ass," I've, I've been called all these things, and, I've taken it, I've never said anything back, you know? (Male, New Mexico).

Nonetheless, there were also a small number of physical and property offenses. Among the most vicious attacks were two cases in which perpetrators bit their victims. In one of these cases, a small piece of the victim's ear was bitten off; in the other, the tip of the victim's tongue was lost. The most extreme violence, however, occurred at the Wisconsin boat landings during the spear fishing conflict in the closing years of the twentieth century. Many participants shared some remarkable tales of their experiences at the time. This one is typical of those stories:

> I was out by the boat landing one night where there was over a thousand people chanting racial things; it got so they wouldn't allow our boats to come off the lake, so we had to take our trucks around, and boat trailers, to

another landing. And I said, well, I'll take one, and another guy too. We did our ceremonies and everything before we left, and we did our water ceremonies when we were there. The stories that came out of that, especially the ones . . . how people would prepare themselves to be there at night. There was spear guns, there was pipe bombs, there was airguns, there was slingshots. One day we were setting the nets and they were throwing rocks and they were shooting, shooting wrist rockets, slingshots with ball bearings. One hit Sarah in her side, and knocked her to the bottom of the boat. I got hit too (Wisconsin, male).

Racial violence and the potential for racial violence are in fact normative in Native American communities and reservation border towns (Perry, 2006; forthcoming). It has become an institutionalized mechanism for establishing boundaries, both social and physical. Violence is one means by which to remind Native Americans where they do and don't belong. As one participant remarked,

The Crow people have it in their heart that just by walking down the street, or seeing him in the wrong place, if they're alone especially and don't know anyone, or if they've been drinking or whatever, and they see Anglos that have been drinking, they don't know if there's going to be violence. They always have it in their heart that there just might be (Montana, male).

This recognition of the risk of racial violence seemed to be endemic to the Native American experience in virtually every community. This is clear, first, in the very frequency and consistency of harassment and violence. Rarely was it described as a "one off" affair that touched them once and never again. As the above quote suggests, the expectation was that, in the presence of non-Native Americans, they were vulnerable to harassment and attack:

It's always there. I don't want to say it's a norm, but we get so used to it, we never know what's coming next, or where it's coming from. That's what it's like to be an Indian around here (Minnesota, male).

However, even in the most extreme cases, violence against Native Americans remains unmarked and unremarkable. In part, this is itself a hallmark of the normativity of violence: it is so constant, so deeply embedded in American Indian lives that it hardly warrants reporting. More significant, however, is the fact that victims see little use in registering complaints with an unsympathetic white justice system, or even with tribal law enforcement authorities. In other words, many participants pointed to what they saw as a law enforcement response that was indifferent at best, violent at worst. This is the heart of the current analysis.

Overview of the Book

Chapter 2: Racialized Policing

In this chapter, I situate the specific experiences of Native Americans within the broader context of the uneasy relationship between minorities and police generally. "Policing race" has generally meant policing those social and physical boundaries across which people of colour are not meant to cross. Collective challenges to the authority of "whiteness" continue to elicit violence on the part of the state, often through the actions of law enforcement agencies. In the contemporary era, this has been especially apparent since the emergence of the civil rights challenges of the 1960s and 1970s.

The civil rights movements spearheaded by people of color initiated a series of challenges and reforms that tested the limits of the prevailing racial order. However, this profound insertion of difference into the currents of political and social life is not without resistance of its own. On the contrary, "strong opposition arose to confront the newfound assertiveness and proliferation of cultural difference that the movement had fostered" (Winant, 1997: 30). While much of the opposition and corresponding violence sprang from the grass-roots, state law enforcement agents also played an integral role. Images of police "dispersing crowds" with fire hoses or tear gas are an indelible part of United States history. Missing and murdered civil rights workers—Native Americas among them—are also part of this legacy of resistance to civil rights advances.

As the contemporary evidence such as the Christopher Commission, and studies of police profiling attests, police remain at the forefront of continued efforts to restrict racial minority communities. They persist in the construction of a racist culture that demonizes and consequently persecutes people of color. It is in this context that we must also understand the policing of Native American communities.

Chapter 3: Colonial Policing and Beyond

The history of EuroAmerican oppression of Native peoples is as old as the history of EuroAmericans. Whether by violence or assimilationist policy, whites have consistently exerted their energies in the ongoing effort to physically or culturally annihilate Native peoples. The origins of the "anti-Indian movement" might be seen in the combined doctrines of Manifest Destiny and European superiority, providing as they did a clear rationale for genocide. And, in fact, genocidal and ethnoviolent practices were often formally or informally institutionalized in state policy. Sadly, the line is not much bolder today. Even in an era in which there is so much talk of Native American communities as "sovereign nations," they continue to be manipulated and weakened by state and federal political realities. This chapter explores the ways in which law enforcement bodies—in different guises—have long played crucial roles in the processes of colonization.

Chapter 4: Over-policing Native American Communities

At one end of the spectrum of policing Native American communities, is the perceived tendency to take very seriously Native American offending, even the potential for offending—hence the very common practice of profiling American Indian drivers. To participants in my study, officers appear eager to explore potential Native American wrong-doing, in contrast to that of their non-Native counterparts. For example, one participant asserted that "when white people get killed everybody wants to know who, and to catch 'em, especially if they think it was an Indian. But not when an Indian gets *killed.*" It is as if police are ready and willing to accept the mythology of the "savage" Indian, and act accordingly.

Beyond this, however, is the added tendency to themselves engage in harassment and violence perpetrated against American Indians. Reports of police misconduct toward Native Americans—running the continuum from name calling to extreme forms of violence—were consistent across my interviews, regardless of location. Like racial violence perpetrated by citizens, police mistreatment of American Indians appears embedded in both the broader culture and the police culture.

Chapter 5: Under-policing Native American Communities

At the other end of the spectrum just described, there is an ongoing tendency to under-enforce the law in Native American communities. In common with many other racial minorities, American Indians perceive police to be, at best, indifferent to their victimization. Common beliefs are that police deny the legitimacy of the victim, or that they fail to act even where violence was imminent or had already occurred. In the case of the former, this is evident in the invocation of stereotypical images of Native Americans ("it's only a drunken Indian," or "just another Indian bitching about nothing"). In addition, there is a common perception that police tended not to intervene or investigate victimization, even in the case of murders or attempted murders.

Chapter 6: Impacts of Disparate Policing

Inevitably, the experiences of Native Americans with police officers shape their perceptions of the brand of justice they can expect. The most common reaction is to cease to engage with law enforcement. In light of participants' perceptions of law enforcement, it comes as no surprise that they fail to report victimization to police. As the visible and uniformed face of the "dominant society," law enforcement agents—even American Indian officers—bear the brunt of this frustration. In light of the perceptions of widespread over- and under-policing, police, they command mistrust rather than confidence. Indians are not likely to freely initiate contact with officers who represent a culture that has so often betrayed them.

Moreover, the perception of recurrent negligence, harassment, and victimization at the hands of police leaves its subjects feeling disempowered. They feel themselves to be without a voice, without an avenue to justice. They feel marginal at best, violently constrained at worst.

For too many American Indians, the perception, if not the reality of police attention and harassment has its intended effect of keeping people in their place. It reinforces the boundaries—social and geographical—across which Native Americans are not meant to cross. It contributes to ongoing withdrawal and isolation; in short, it furthers historical patterns of segregation.

Chapter 7: Policing Differently?

This chapter critically assesses initiatives touted as responses to the racist culture and behaviours of law enforcement generally and in Indian Country specifically. It examines four concrete strategies that have been offered as panaceas to the problems associated with racialized policing: cultural awareness training; community policing; minority recruitment; and tribal policing. Each of these initiatives is fraught with limitations of its own. However, all share the fundamental flaw of remaining locked in Western ideals of social control, and ultimately fail to address the structural supports for the racism that informs the disparate policing of Native American communities.

Notes

1. The results of this survey are discussed in detail in Perry (2002).

Chapter 2
Racialized Policing

The role of the state in policing race is inextricably linked to its role in the politics of identity-making and the construction of difference. In fact, Omi and Winant (1994) make the argument that the state is increasingly the pre-eminent site of racial conflict. The state is implicated in constructing popular notions of identity in racialized terms. Ascendancy—or domination—"which is embedded in religious doctrine and practice, mass media content, wage structures, the design of housing, welfare/taxation policies and so forth" (Connell, 1987: 184) applies as much to the construction of hierarchies of race and ethnicity as it does to class. West and Fenstermaker (1995: 9) remind us that race, along with class and gender, acts as a "mechanism for producing social inequality." Of course, Jim Crow laws are among the strongest historical examples of this racial ordering. But the banning of Affirmative Action legislation—on the grounds that "quotas" are unjust—is a more contemporary expression of the "proper" place of minorities. The state not only holds us accountable to race, but plays a critical role in shaping what it means to do race. Thus, the state serves to both define and maintain what it is to "do difference."

The notion of "race" is not without controversy. The standard debate revolves around whether race is a biological given, or whether it is socially constructed. Here, I assume the latter. Granted, there are identifiable and even visible differences between groups - in terms of hair texture, or skin color for example. Yet these cannot account for the varied life experiences and life chances of different groups. Rather, we must look to the meanings and values assigned—culturally—to these groups to understand their distinct positionalities. In short, it is important to understand that "racialization"—like criminalization as defined in chapter 1—constitutes a conscious process of according place to biological characteristics. Yet through this process, race does become "real" or at least reified by members of a given society. It comes to be seen as an objective and immutable characteristic of all social groups.

By what processes do racial categories become stable and in fact institutionalized? Succinctly, it might be understood as follows:

> Processes of characterization take place through representations (symbols, images), micro-interactions (norms, stereotypes), and social structures through which resources are allocated (Mirchandani and Chan, 2002: 12).

This aligns nicely with my own variant of structured action theory, according to which the social construction of difference can be seen as developed through the operation of both structure and agency:

> Racial categorization, then, represents the placing of racial groups within unequal relations of dominance and subordination. Moreover, the resultant hierarchy—while the object of resistance—is nonetheless continually reconstituted in and through multiple social forms: discourse, power, policy, and patterns of ownership, for example. In other words, a web of racial projects is informed by interlocking cultural and structural forms (Perry, 2001: 91).

Significantly, Mirchandi and Chan (2002) draw a connection between the mutually constitutive processes of racialization and criminalization, referring to the "merging" of the two. In particular, they argue that racialized communities have been over-criminalized. Similarly, Holdaway's (1996; Holdaway and Barron, 1997) extensive work on black police officers in the U.K. explicitly examines the "racialisation" of British police, by which he means the "ways in which 'race' is constructed within the relationships between the police and black and Asian people" (Holdaway, 1996: 23). Thus, he, too, links the process of racialization with the process of criminalization.

At the forefront of efforts to maintain these patterns are the police. Indeed, Gunnar Myrdal's observations of police-black relations in the 1930s and 1940s remain disturbingly accurate seven decades later. Writing in 1944, he stated that "The Negro's most important public contact is with the policeman. He is the personification of white authority in the Negro community" (Myrdal, 1995 [1944]: 535). The machinery of law enforcement is responsible for the enforcement of the formal and informal social order, which is shaped by what are often discriminatory laws. The Black Codes and Jim Crow laws are the historical predecessors to crack cocaine sentencing principles, for example. Moreover, it is no accident that the earliest formalized police bodies in North America were constituted as slave patrols, with the legitimate authority to seek and apprehend escaped slaves as a means of maintaining their servitude (Bass, 2001; Taylor Greene, 2003). Thus it fell to these earliest patrols to closely and forcefully guard the subordinate place of African Americans. Even now, one hundred and fifty years after the Emancipation Proclamation, racialized minorities continue to be disproportionately and disparately subject to the attention of the police.

In the contemporary era, the use of state power—*viz* law enforcement—has been especially apparent since the emergence of the civil rights challenges of the 1960s and 1970s.

> As minority legal oppression became increasingly unbearable, particularly when minority members were literally denied control of their own communities, many rebelled. The ensuing racial protests, or as they were viewed by the dominant majority, "riots," and their suppression led to a shocking series of brutal, violent and lawless acts by law enforcement representatives throughout the country (Mann, 1993: 127).

Indeed, "race riots" like those characteristic of the "long hot summers" of the mid-1960s were often responses to what was seen as unfettered violence perpetrated by police on people of colour. Even as recently as 1980 in Miami, and of course Los Angeles in 1992, urban riots inspired by perceived lack of protection afforded minority communities provide testimony to the hostile relationship between people of colour and police.

The civil rights movements spearheaded by people of color initiated a series of challenges and reforms that tested the limits of the prevailing racial order. However, this profound insertion of difference into the currents of political and social life was not without resistance of its own. On the contrary, "strong opposition arose to confront the newfound assertiveness and proliferation of cultural difference that the movement had fostered" (Winant, 1997: 30). While much of the opposition and corresponding violence sprang from the grass-roots, state law enforcement agents also played an integral role. Images of police "dispersing crowds" with fire hoses or tear gas are an indelible part of United States history. Missing and murdered civil rights workers—black, white, Jewish, Native American and Latino—are also part of this legacy of police suppression of civil rights advances. In 1967 alone, eighty-three people, mostly black, were killed, and hundreds more injured at the hands of police. As the 1960s proved, collective challenges to the authority of "whiteness" frequently elicit violence on the part of the state, often through the actions of law enforcement agencies. In fact, formalized police forces emerge only

> where the conditions are right—where there is a substantial degree of inequality among the population, for example, where many relationships are distant and impersonal, where lifestyles struggle for dominance, where unemployment, homelessness and isolation are widespread, and where people have few alternatives by which to handle their conflicts (Black, 1980: 40).

In short, police and police violence are crucial to the maintenance of a particular social order in the context of threats from below. For example, at the forefront of state harassment and violence against minorities throughout the 1960s and 1970s was the FBI's Counter Intelligence Program—COINTELPRO. This institutional policy was initiated in 1941, largely to eliminate Communists. However, in the 1960s it was relaunched with the expanded mandate to disrupt and neutralize "dissident" groups, specifically, those of Native Americans, blacks, and Puerto Rican *independentistas* (Churchill, 1997; Messerschmidt, 1983; Churchill and Vander Wall, 1990). A 1968 memorandum, for example, encouraged COINTELPRO agents to

> prevent the coalition of militant black nationalist groups . . . prevent militant black nationalist groups and leaders from gaining respectability . . . prevent the rise of a black "messiah" who could unify and electrify the militant black nationalist movement. Malcolm X might have been such a "messiah;" he is the martyr of the movement today (cited in Churchill and Vander Wall, 1990: 58).

In short, COINTELPRO was designed to prevent or eliminate the construction of collective oppositional racial identities. With respect to black activists, this meant that the Black Panther Party (BPP) and the Nation of Islam were singled out for special attention. Late in 1969, for example, agents broke into the home of BPP activist Fred Hampton, killed two members and injured several others. This was typical of the COINTELPRO activities, with the result that

> During the Nixon era, and during its adjunct Ford administration, hundreds of black organizers were murdered, destabilized or imprisoned. Nearly every case is now traceable to government intelligence sources and outright assassination and frame-ups. . . . The attack on Indian demonstrators and particularly on American Indian Movement activists was brutal and grisly, with a far greater ratio of deaths and imprisonments than any other movement (Ortiz, 1981: 12).

As Ortiz reports, the American Indian Movement (AIM) was also a favored target of police repression. Organized to resist the allocation and exploitation of Native American lands, and the more generalized oppression of Native peoples, AIM was fated to be seen as a dissident group which threatened the racial order. Nowhere did the campaign turn more deadly than on the Pine Ridge Reservation in South Dakota. AIM took a leading role in challenging a proposed transfer of mineral rich land back to the federal government. In response, local police departments, the FBI and a tribal ranger group—the GOONsquad—mustered massive resources and ammunition against the Native American organizers. In the end, dozens of Native Americans had been killed, hundreds more injured by gunfire, beatings, and cars forced off the road (Messerschmidt, 1983). This contemporary "Indian war" took a tremendous toll:

> Even if only documented political deaths are counted, the yearly murder rate on the Pine Ridge Reservation between 1 March 1973 and 1 March 1976 was 170 per 100,000. By comparison, Detroit, the reputed "murder capital of the United States," had a rate of 20.2 per 100,000 in 1974. The U.S. average was 9.7 per 100,000 (Johnson and Maestas, 1979: 83-84).

What these patterns of police brutality illustrate is that violence is an appropriate means with which to confront counter-hegemonic racial mobilization. When black or Native or Puerto Ricans organize to upset the racial balance, it is acceptable to put them back in their place quite forcibly. Those who cross the political, social or cultural boundaries are legitimate victims of racial violence. So, too, are those who cross geographic boundaries. Those who "don't belong" are also subject to the coercive actions of law enforcement agents, in a way that parallels the localized "move-in" violence perpetrated by other offenders.

The Legacy of Racialized Justice:
Failed Commissions

One way to assess the limited progress made in terms of police-minority relations is to trace the many commissions that have investigated police misconduct. The first national inquiry of this type was the Wickersham Commission of 1931, so named in honor of its Chair, George W. Wickersham, former U.S. attorney general. Among the other members of the commission were Roscoe Pound, dean of Harvard Law School; Newton Baker, a Progressive era reformer; and Frank J. Loesch, leader of the Chicago Crime Commission, and Al Capone's nemesis.

This was the first national inquiry of its kind in the United States. The scope of the commission was decidedly broad, and resulted in fourteen distinct reports covering the following areas of inquiry: Prohibition; Enforcement of the Prohibition Laws of the United States; Criminal Statistics; Prosecution; Enforcement of the Deportation Laws of the United States; the Child Offender in the Federal System of Justice and the Federal Courts; Criminal Procedure; Penal Institutions, Probation, and Parole; Crime and the Foreign Born; the Cost of Crime; the Causes of Crime (two volumes); and the Police. The latter report, otherwise known as the *Report on Lawlessness in Law Enforcement* is of particular interest here, as it did shed some light on the disparate treatment of racialized minorities of the day, albeit indirectly. The Report is especially critical of what it referred to as the "third degree," or what we might today refer to as police brutality. The Report concludes that "the third degree brutalizes the police, hardens the prisoner against society, and lowers the esteem in which the administration of justice is held by the public" (Wickersham Commission, 1931: 5). Clearly, the roots of police misconduct run deep, both culturally and historically.

It would be four decades before law enforcement would again come under such close public scrutiny. While some cities and states engaged in inquiries into policing, the next national foray into the closed ranks of law enforcement emerged in 1967 in the form of the President's Commission on Law Enforcement and the Administration of Justice. The final report acknowledged—almost grudgingly it seems—that black and Latino/a hostility toward police was commonly rooted in the reality that "too many policemen do misunderstand and are indifferent to minority-group aspirations, attitudes and customs, and that incidents involving physical or verbal mistreatment do occur and do contribute to the resentment against police that some minority-group members feel" (President's Commission on Law Enforcement and the Administration of Justice, 1968: 100). As correctives, the Commission recommended a slate of "Community Relations Programs" intended to enhance the relationship between police and urban minority communities.

The 1968 Kerner Commission was much more critical of police engagement in minority communities. Like the Wickersham Commission before it, the Kerner Commission (formally the National Advisory

Committee on Social Disorders) had a broad mandate covering social, political, economic, and civil arenas. Unlike the Wickersham Commission, however, it explicitly addressed the racial dynamics of inequities in these areas. Called by President Johnson in the midst of successive race riots across the country, it was the final report of this commission that penned the now famous phrase "Our nation is moving toward two societies, one black, one white—separate and unequal." At the heart of the commission's findings were sweeping indictments of police bias and misconduct directed toward minority communities, and especially black communities:

> The police are not merely a "spark" factor. To some Negroes police have come to symbolize white power, white racism and white repression. And the fact is that many police do reflect and express these white attitudes. The atmosphere of hostility and cynicism is reinforced by a widespread belief among Negroes in the existence of police brutality and in a "double standard" of justice and protection—one for Negroes and one for whites (Kerner, 1968).

Indeed, so central was the problem of racialized policing seen to be that chapter 11 was devoted entirely to the conflict between black communities and the police. In the end, the Commission made seven concrete recommendations with respect to policing black communities:

- Review police operations in the ghetto to ensure proper conduct by police officers, and eliminate abrasive practices.
- Provide more adequate police protection to the ghetto residents to eliminate their high sense of insecurity, and the belief of many Negro citizens in the existence of a dual standard of law enforcement.
- Establish fair and effective mechanisms for the redress of grievances against the police, and other municipal employees.
- Develop and adopt policy guidelines to assist officers in making critical decisions in areas where police conduct can create tension.
- Develop and use innovative programs to ensure widespread community support for law enforcement.
- Recruit more Negros into the regular police force, and review promotion policies to ensure fair promotion for Negro officers.
- Establish a "Community Service Officer" program to attract ghetto youths between the ages of 17 and 21 to police work. These junior officers would perform duties in ghetto neighborhoods, but would not have full police authority. The federal government should provide support equal to 90 percent of the costs of employing CSOs on the basis of one for every ten regular officers.

An array of media and academic articles in 1998—30 year retrospectives—bemoaned the fact that little had changed, that poor, black, Latino, and Native American communities still suffered discriminatory treatment at the hands of racist police officers and racist police practices. Of course, their assessments had been made in the aftermath of the LA riots which gave rise to a more recent inquiry: the Christopher Commission of 1991. While focusing primarily on the problems embedded within the LAPD, the report's findings were arguably generalizable to police departments nationwide. The report was very explicit in its recognition and censure of widespread racist attitudes and behaviors within the police department—behavior which it argued was condoned by the failure of leadership to intervene. Even the officers polled believed racism to be endemic to the force—over 25% of officers agreed both that racism threatened the relationship between police and the racial minority communities they were meant to serve, and that racist attitudes spilled over into the use of excessive force against minority group members.

Direct evidence of the prejudice of police officers was drawn from Mobile Digital Terminal (MDT) transmissions. Officers made free use of racial epithets and analogies, as in the following: "sounds like monkey slapping time," and "I would love to drive down Slauson with a flamethrower . . . we would have a barbecue." (Christopher Commission, xii). Hearing testimony confirmed that such attitudes translated into action in the field, as officers reported frequent incidents of verbal harassment, intimidation, and use of excessive force against blacks and Latinos.

Institutional Racism: The "Canteen Culture"

That racism continues to be endemic to the police culture is self-evident, as is the fact that this infects the ways in which members of racialized minority groups are treated by police officers. The manifestations of this racism are many and varied, ranging from the use of derogatory language and epithets at one extreme, to brutal assaults on ethnic minority individuals at the other. Underlying the array of activities, of course, are racist and stereotypical mindsets that legitimate the hostility and discrimination directed toward particular groups. In addressing the Stephen Lawrence Inquiry in the UK, the president of the UK Association of Chief Police Officers clearly acknowledged that the sort of institutional racism identified by the Report derived from

> the racism which is inherent in society which shapes our attitudes and behaviour. Those attitudes and behaviours are then reinforced and shaped by the culture of the organization that the person works for. In the police services there is a distinct tendency for officers to stereotype people. That creates problems in a number of areas, but particularly in the way officers deal with Black people (MacPherson, 1999: para.6.50).

The British literature uses the provocative term "canteen culture" to describe the often racist and typically insular nature of the police officer's world.

American scholars point to similar patterns, wherein the distinct—and socially distant—police workplace is reflected in "a closed system of ideas, a reluctance to question the statements of actions of fellow officers, and 'matter of fact prejudices' that are reinforced through customs, rituals, and a shared language" (Fagan and Davies, 2000: 500). More prosaically referred to in this country as "the subculture of policing," it nonetheless describes the same organizational structures whereby everyday racism informs relationships between white and non-white, officers and non-officers.

Similarly, a review by Her Majesty's Inspectorate of the Constabulary (HMIC) (1997) of police and race relations makes the claim that there is "a direct and vital link between internal culture and the way people are treated and external performance." Such observations are supported by the scholarly evidence linking racist attitudes among police officers to their (mis)treatment of people of color (Rowe, 2004; Bowling and Phillips, 2002; Holdaway, 1996). The cultural myths which have come to signify people of color inform police violence against minorities. They provide the context within which law enforcement officers can rationalize their own relational enactment of white masculinity through brutal acts. Skin color alone marks the "other" as deviant, criminal, potentially violent. That race matters to police in their efforts to manage identity is apparent in Cornel West's (1994) experiences with police: "Years ago, while driving from New York to teach at Williams College, I was stopped on fake charges of trafficking cocaine. I told the police officer I was a professor of religion, he replied, 'Yeh, and I'm the Flying Nun. Let's go, nigger'" (xv). There is no room for positive imagery of blacks when "black men, by their very existence, are valid suspects" (Watts, 1993: 241).

Butler's (1993) examination of the Rodney King beating reveals the normativity of the assumption of black pathology. The black body is already and always inscribed as a threat to the safety and sanctity of whiteness. People of color may, at any time, cross the appropriate physical and social boundaries which otherwise insulate them from whites. This is where the police enter; they are situated as guardians of these borders, charged to "protect whiteness against violence, where violence is the imminent action of that black male body" (Butler, 1993: 18). Police violence is legitimate in this schema—it is a defensive act. Such violence is a safe display of both the "whiteness" and the "aggressive masculinity" of the perpetrator. While police violence against minorities recasts the latter in demonized terms, it attests to the perpetrators' solidarity with their predominantly white male peers.

Consequently, police violence is especially likely to occur where the victims have forgotten their "appropriate" place in the racial order. The loss of place may even be geographical as well as social, hence the likelihood of police harassment of people of color in predominantly white neighborhoods. Minority women are not immune, either, as is evident in Laura Fishman's (1998: 116) experiences:

> I was deemed suspicious enough to be stopped simply because I was a black woman. This form of police harassment always occurred whenever I walked in white, affluent neighborhoods. Not only was I rudely questioned about my purpose for walking in these neighborhoods, frequently I was required to give proof that I was not a prostitute, heroin addict or maniac.

Police brutality is most likely in situations wherein minority individuals or communities are attempting to construct oppositional racial identities. These efforts challenge the marginal or subordinate position which has been assigned to them, and which is expected of them. Harassment and violence become resources by which to restore the balance.

On the street, these dynamics play themselves out in conflicts between police and minority individuals who assume an antagonistic or resistant stance. It is not surprising that in communities where minority youth are routinely stopped, searched and questioned for no reason other than the color of their skin, that these same youth are hostile towards police. In an attempt to empower themselves relative to the uniformed force of white racism, they do away with the deference that is expected of them as members of subordinate races. The legacy of indifference, hostility and brutality toward minority communities "breeds consequences. When any minority group experiences injustice at the hands of the dominant society, anger, frustration and agony are bred" (Boldt, 1993: 60). So, too, are the roots of resistance sown. Minority youth respond to the context of brutalization with attempts to gain both racial and gender recognition through challenging or confrontational behavior. On the one hand, such behavior serves notice to police that the individual in question does not accept his or her subordination. On the other hand, for males especially, it is a peer display of one's toughness, fearlessness, and solidarity. While this may gain respect from one's peers, it may enrage police officers who see resistance as a threat to their (racial) authority. Consequently, they believe that their use of force is justified in the interests of showing the "suspect" his "place." Rodney King's resistance to police apprehension, for example, was read as justification enough for his beating. So begins the deadly cycle in which racial politics gives rise to oppositional and reactionary confrontations. Each "side" is consumed with enacting a racial identity that is empowered and recognized.

Moreover, even in the absence of blatant resistance, police commonly respond to people of color—victims, witnesses, and suspects alike—with incivility if not outright violence (Hamilton and Sinclair, 1991). Nor is it only in times of political agitation that law enforcement differentially polices minority communities. Rather, selective enforcement is an ongoing pattern of response. Black's (1980: 3) reference to the variations in the application of law along several dimensions of social space highlights this tendency:

> These include a vertical dimension, arising from an uneven distribution of wealth; a horizontal dimension, described by the distribution of people in relation to each other; a cultural dimension, pertaining to the symbolic aspect of social life; a corporate dimension, referring to the capacity of people for collective action; and a normative dimension, determined by the distribution of authority and social control.

On all dimensions, people of color are at a distinct disadvantage, thus allowing the differential police response to victims and suspects alike. The remainder of the chapter details the ways in which these "differential responses" are manifest in both over- and under-policing of minority communities. As the following sections will demonstrate, this dichotomy represents an important distinction. The two strategies constitute a dual assault on the rights and freedoms of already marginalized, often stigmatized groups. In the final report of the Canadian Inquiry into the Administration of Justice and Aboriginal People, Hamilton and Sinclair (2001: 595) articulate both the differences and the links between the two:

> Over-policing generally results from the imposition of police control on individual or community activities at a level unlikely to occur in the dominant society. Under-policing usually results from a lack of preventive and supportive police services. While the possibility of simultaneously experiencing those two problems may appear unlikely at first glance, both arise because police forces are not under Aboriginal community direction, and [police] likely do not know community priorities or cultural assumptions.

Both forms of police (mis)treatment of racialized minority groups leave them vulnerable and devoid of the protections afforded white citizens. On the one hand, over-enforcement renders people of color objects of law enforcement. It implies that the "task of police is to keep them under control" (Williams and Murphy, 1990: 28). On the other hand, under-policing deprives them of civil and legal protections, implying that "the police have little responsibility for protecting them from crime within their communities" (Williams and Murphy, 1990: 28).

Over-policing, or selective enforcement, takes many forms, ranging from verbal abuse, to harassment and disproportionate surveillance, discriminatory patterns of arrest, and to excessive use of physical and deadly force. The other side of the coin—under-enforcement—might also be understood to constitute selective protection, wherein police manifest delayed response to calls for assistance, failure to take complaints seriously, and failure to protect citizens who are members of racialized groups.

Selective Enforcement

As noted above, at one end of the spectrum of police engagement with racialized communities is the tendency to over-police. This is especially evident in racial profiling, harassment and other related forms of "stop and search." This, too, can be traced back in part to stereotyped views wherein "the crimes of the individual came to be seen as the crimes of the community" (Whitfield, 2004: 158). Whitfield's observation reflects the apparent reality of law enforcement assumptions about the connection between race and criminality, assumptions that are ultimately used to justify selective intervention. The first faulty assumption is that it is members of minority communities that commit the majority of crimes, and thus warrant greater scrutiny. The second and related assumption is that most members of these same groups engage in criminal activity, and thus racial profiling is likely to result in a "hit," i.e., the discovery of wrongdoing (Leadership

Conference on Civil Rights, 2005).

Bowling and Phillips (2002) cite both official Home Office data and academic studies that underscore the broad disparities in the use of stop and search. One Home Office (2000) report found that blacks were stopped and searched five times more often than whites, while Asians were stopped relatively less, but still were still more likely to be stopped than whites. A cumulative report four years later shows that the trend is holding:

> Black people and those of Mixed origin were more likely to be stopped than White people, whether on foot or in cars. Asian people were more likely to be stopped in vehicles than White people in vehicles, but no more likely to be stopped on foot. A detailed study of policing in London found not only that Black people were more likely than others to be stopped, but they faced a higher risk of multiple stops over the course of a year (Home Office, 2004: 14).

And the trend certainly holds for the United States as well, particularly under the influence of widespread zero tolerance policing, or quality of life policing, which both involve draconian crack downs on relatively low level offences. Mayor Giuliani's New York City is probably the most (in)famous case in point. Here, where blacks and Hispanics each made up a quarter of the population, they accounted for one-half and one-third, respectively, of those stopped on the street; the proportions were even more extreme in predominantly white neighborhoods, where people of color "did not belong" (Bass, 2001).

The stop and search practices noted above are part and parcel of a broader pattern of behaviors now known collectively as racial profiling. Amnesty International (2004) and the Ontario Human Rights Commission (2003) provide useful definitions of the term:

> Racial profiling occurs when law enforcement agents rely solely on race, ethnicity, national origin, or religion in deciding whom to target for criminal investigation (Amnesty International, 2004).

> any action undertaken for reasons of safety, security or public protection that relies on stereotypes about race, colour, ethnicity, ancestry, religion, or place of origin rather than on reasonable suspicion, to single out an individual for greater scrutiny or different treatment (OHRC, 2003: 6).

Both reports also recognize that racial profiling occurs in multiple and diverse contexts. Contemporary scholarship has tended to focus on vehicular profiling, although this has begun to shift with the increased tendency to profile those deemed to be of Middle Eastern descent in the aftermath of the September 11 attacks. Consider the following illustrations of the different forms of profiling:

- *While driving:* A young African-American schoolteacher reports being routinely pulled over in his suburban neighborhood in San Carlos, California, where only five other African-American families live. Native Americans in Oklahoma report being routinely stopped by police because of the tribal tags displayed on their cars. In Texas, a Muslim student of South Asian ancestry is pulled over and asked by police if he is carrying any dead bodies or bombs.

- *While walking*: In Seattle, Washington, a group of Asian-American youths are detained on a street corner by police for forty-five minutes on an allegation of jaywalking. While a sergeant ultimately ordered the officer in question to release them, the young people say they saw whites repeatedly crossing the same street in an illegal manner without being stopped.

- *While traveling through airports*: An eight-year-old Muslim boy from Tulsa, Oklahoma was reportedly separated from his family while airport security officials searched him and dismantled his Boy Scout pinewood derby car. He is now routinely stopped and searched at airports.

- *While shopping*: In New York City, an African-American woman shopping for holiday presents was stopped by security at a major department store. She showed the guards her receipts. Nonetheless, she was taken to a holding cell in the building where every other suspect she saw was a person of color. She was subjected to threats and a body search. She was allowed to leave without being charged three hours later, but was not allowed to take her purchases.

- *While at home*: A Latino family in a Chicago suburb was reportedly awoken at 4:50 A.M. on the day after Father's Day by nine building inspectors and police officers who prohibited the family from getting dressed or moving about. The authorities reportedly proceeded to search the entire house to find evidence of overcrowding. Enforcement of the zoning ordinance, which was used to justify the search, was reportedly targeted at the rapidly-growing Latino population.

- *While traveling to and from places of worship*: A Muslim imam from the Dallas area reports being stopped and arrested by police upon leaving a mosque after an outreach event. Officers stopped him, searched his vehicle, arrested him for expired vehicle tags, and confiscated his computer (Amnesty International, 2004).

Such practices are disturbingly common, and affect people from multiple communities, including Native Americans, Asian Americans, Hispanic Americans, African Americans, Arab Americans, American Muslims, as well as visitors to this country. Amnesty International estimates that in the region of thirty-two million Americans have already been victims of racial profiling, and that many more at a high risk of being subjected to future racial profiling during their lifetime. Yet the risk is not evenly distributed, as table 2.1 indicates.

Table 2.1
National Estimate of Racial Profiling

Race	Total Population %	Profiling Rate %
Black (non-Hispanic)	34	47
Hispanic	35	23
Asian (non-Hispanic)	10	11
Multi-racial (non-Hispanic)	5	11
White	195	3

Adapted from Amnesty International (2004: 1).

Oddly, it is only in the last decade or so that social scientists have come to attend to this "new" crisis facing people of color. In fact, Russell-Brown (2004) suggests that our attention to the relatively infrequent incidents of extreme police brutality has overshadowed the more common, more far-reaching incidents of "routine stops" that characterize petit apartheid on American streets, in airports, and at border crossings. Nonetheless, in the short period of time that scholars have been attending to racial profiling, the presence of the problem has been strongly documented in dozens of studies across the United States (Cole, 1999; Harris, 1999). A recent Leadership Conference on Civil Rights (LCCR, 2002) report catalogs just a few of the most significant reports and their findings with respect to highway profiling, specifically, including the following:

- A U.S. Department of Justice report on police contacts with the public concluded that in 1999, African Americans were 20 percent more likely to be stopped than White Americans, and 50 percent more likely than Whites to have experienced more than one stop. Police were more than twice as likely to search an African American or Hispanic driver than a White driver.
- In the three-year period from January 1995 to December 1997, Blacks comprised more than 70 percent of the drivers stopped and searched by the Maryland State Highway Patrol, although they made up only 17.5 percent of the overall drivers (and overall speeders). These disparities were explained by a state document called the "Criminal Intelligence Report," which contained an explicit policy targeting Black motorists.
- A study of traffic stops on the New Jersey Turnpike between 1988-1991 found that Blacks were 35 percent of those stopped, though only 13.5 percent of the cars on the turnpike had a Black occupant and Blacks were only 15 percent of all traffic violators. A 1999 State Attorney General's Report studying Turnpike stops and

searches in 1997-1998 concluded that almost 80 percent of searches involved Blacks and other minorities.

- In the early 1990s, an investigation of the practices of the Volusia County, Florida Sheriff's Department revealed that although Blacks or Hispanics were only five percent of the drivers on a portion of I-95 that ran through the county, they were nearly 70 percent of drivers stopped on that stretch of highway. Blacks and Hispanics were not only stopped more than Whites, they were also stopped for longer periods of time than Whites.

Of course, post-September 11, the complexion of racial profiling, so to speak, has changed dramatically. To that point, it was largely blacks and Latinos that bore the brunt of police suspicion. In the shift in priorities from the "war on drugs" to the "war on terrorism," those perceived by authorities to be Muslim or broadly of Middle Eastern origin are similarly at risk of ongoing police surveillance and harassment (LCCR, 2002; CAIR, 2005, 2004). Not hundreds, but thousands of Middle Eastern people—mostly men—have been detained by federal authorities. Additionally, the 2001 Council on American Islamic Relations (CAIR) report lists a number of reports filed with them in which federal agents from the FBI, INS, IRS, and even the Secret Service "approached" or "contacted" Arabs and Muslims, often with no explanation for the contact. A few examples:

- An FBI agent contacted one man saying he wanted to talk to him about someone else but would not explain what was at issue.
- A founder of an Islamic organization reported that an FBI agent wanted to talk about another organization and another individual but would not explain why.
- An Algerian imam (prayer leader) was approached by the Secret Service, who said that they had received a letter about him, but that there was no problem and would be no additional contact. They would not explain what was in the letter, who sent it, or why it instigated contact.
- A man claimed that FBI agents followed him, made surprise visits to his house, and asked his neighbors about his "terrorist activities."
- A community leader was asked to meet with FBI agents with no explanation.
- Two FBI agents came unannounced to an immigrant man's house, asked him about his residency status, and asked for personal photographs, again with no explanation.

Equally disturbing are the activities of local law enforcement agents. They have followed the lead of federal agencies in their increased use of racial profiling and harassment of "suspicious" individuals. Hundreds of such reports have come in to Arab Anti-Defamation Committee and CAIR, ranging from unjustified highway stops, to police harassment, to failure to take seriously complaints of civilian harassment. By November 2001, the ADC had already logged hundreds of such complaints; by January 2002, CAIR had recorded over two hundred cases of police profiling or harassment, and nearly the same number of cases of airport profiling. Among the incidents reported are the following illustrative examples:

- Westbury, NY—police stormed the house of a Muslim man with their guns drawn, and dragged him out of bed. He was taken outside and interrogated, while other officers searched his home. He was not shown a search warrant and was not charged with any crime.
- Fairfax, VA—a Muslim man took his pregnant wife to the hospital because of severe bleeding. She was made to wait while others were seen ahead of her. When the husband complained, the hospital staff called the Fairfax police. The officer made him stand outside while his wife was taken in to be treated. The man was told he would be arrested if he didn't leave.
- Rhode Island—state police and federal agents pulled two Sikhs and an elderly Muslim man off of an Amtrak train, without provocation. One—a telecommunications specialist originally from India—was detained and questioned for six hours until it was determined that he was not a "terrorist." However, he was charged with a misdemeanour for possession of a weapon—a six inch ceremonial knife.
- Longview, TX—A Muslim man who had been awaiting his labor certification before the law was changed was picked up by officers who arrested him and forced him to sign a paper calling for his deportation. He was told that he had thirty seconds to sign it or he would be held in jail for a year.

Disparate stop and search practices have significant consequences for police-community relations. They further alienate the affected communities, exacerbating historical trends. Ultimately, this has consequences for the ability of police to do their job, as it fosters unwillingness to cooperate.

Another reason for concern about the abuse of police stop and search authority has to do with the interaction itself. Research suggests that disproportionate stops and searches of members of minority groups contribute to their subsequent over-representation as arrestees, and as victims of police violence. The LCCR (2002) report noted earlier cites David Harris' characterization of the self-fulfilling prophecy created by the practices associated with race-based stops and searches:

> Because police will look for drug crime among black drivers, they will find it disproportionately among black drivers. More blacks will be arrested, prosecuted, convicted, and jailed, thereby reinforcing the idea that blacks constitute the majority of drug offenders. This will provide a continuing motive and justification for stopping more black drivers as a rational way of using resources to catch the most criminals.

Statistics in England and Wales bear out this trend, in that an arrest is more likely to be forthcoming for Blacks and Asians who are stopped and searched than is the case for their white counterparts (Rowe, 2004). Bowling and Phillips (2002) report that Blacks are typically four times as likely as whites to be arrested, and that Asians are also disproportionately affected. The problem has been exacerbated in recent years by the questionable tactics associated with the war on drugs. For example, while blacks account for about 12% of the U.S. population and just a little over 10% of drug users, they are dramatically over-represented as a proportion of those arrested (one-third) and convicted (two-thirds) for drug offenses (Bass, 2001: 166). Moreover, it is not necessarily the case that the arrests confirm the police officers' "suspicions." In fact, far too often the subsequent charge is unrelated to any predicate offence. Rather, it reflects the "fraught nature of the interface," that is, the arrest emerges out of the dynamics of the interaction between officer and "offender," as when the suspect fails to convey the proper attitude of compliance (Bowling and Phillips, 2002).

The alternative potential outcome of police stop and search—police use of violence—has long been a focus of popular and scholarly attention in the United States. This is not surprising given the persistence of the problem: "Like clockwork, every few years, our first brush with police brutality is linked with a contemporary case of police abuse" (Russell-Brown, 2004: 55). Russell-Brown goes on to cite a Department of Justice survey that documents the disproportionate impact of police brutality against people of color. The Mollen Commission Report in 1994 profiling police violence in New York City, and the more recent investigation of widespread brutality and harassment in the Rampart division of the Los Angeles both demonstrate that such abuses of police authority are not the isolated outcomes of "bad apples," but that they are systemic problems that permeate policing.

Selective Protection

Interestingly, both of these tactics—police brutality and racial profiling—constitute over-policing, that is, disproportionate attention to real or perceived or potential criminal activity suspected of racial minorities. However, black, Latino/a, and other racialized community members are equally critical of the ways in which perceived police hostility toward them manifests in under-policing. Black (1980) reminds us that, while discrimination is generally taken to refer to the tendency toward harsher treatment of people of color viz. white people, this oversimplifies police behavior. In fact, Black argues, police are as likely to disregard the complaints of people of color. So for example, "Wealthier whites who offend blacks are expected to be treated leniently, while poor blacks who offend other poor blacks are expected to be handled with less severity than whites" (Black, 1980: 13). Randall Kennedy (1997: 29) concurs, stating that deliberately withholding protection from black victimization is among the most "destructive" manifestations of racial oppression and injustice.

With respect to under-enforcement, the Canadian and Australian bodies of literature are especially informative. Cunneen (2001) and Neugebauer (1999) speak to the tendency of law enforcement officers to take less seriously the victimization of Aboriginal people—less seriously than their offending, and less seriously than the victimization of white people. Cunneen (2001) draws particular attention to "selective policing" as it affects Aboriginal women who are victims of domestic violence. There is some evidence of such perceptions in the UK as well. The HMIC (1997) review of police-community race relations found that the people whom they consulted "inevitably saw racial bias in late attendance at scenes, indifferent service on arrival, and lack of cultural awareness" (para. 2.31). The message received is that they are not worth the time or energy devoted to other "worthier" constituents.

In the United States, selective under-enforcement historically facilitated both the unfettered rape of black women and the lynching of black men. Neither the law nor law enforcement authorities recognized the sexual assault of black women as constituting "criminal" behavior, especially when victims were slaves raped by their male owners. This was not a crime, but the legitimate "use" of the slave-holders "property." Not only was his behavior not criminalized; it was seen as his right. Even where black women were raped by black men, this constituted criminally enforceable behavior only to the extent that it was a form of trespass on the owner's property; the violation was against him, not the female victim.

While law enforcement passively enabled the rape of black women, they were often more directly complicit in the lynching of black men. Police officers were as likely to open the cell door for the vigilante mob as they were to protect it. They were typically members of the celebratory crowd of spectators witnessing the lynching. Rarely, however, did they intervene to put a stop to the mob violence, however brutal it became. The vigilantes were only right, after all, to mete out suitable justice to the black rapist preying on their white women. Police could only applaud and support efforts to reinforce "appropriate" raced and gendered boundaries.

Contemporary parallels are to be found in both the failure to protect men and women of color from racial violence, and women of color from intimate partner violence. Police officers set the stage for racially motivated violence by acts of omission, or failure to act on behalf of minority victims. Racial violence is explicitly condoned when police fail to investigate or lay charges when victims report assaults motivated by racial bias. It is little wonder, in light of police action and inaction, that victims of hate crime are reluctant to report victimization. Typically, only between 15% and 20% of such victimizations are ever reported to police (Berrill and Herek, 1992: Levin, 1999), largely because the victims anticipate either lack of concern, or some form of secondary victimization. As indicated throughout this chapter, this might take the form of hostility, further abuse, or inaction. This disempowers victims. They perceive themselves to be without legal redress. Conversely, it empowers perpetrators, by signifying the validity and acceptability of their actions. Police abuse and police neglect are enabling; they communicate to the public at large that, by virtue of their racial transgressions, people of color forfeit civil protections. Like other marginalized groups, people of color are implicitly and explicitly designated "assailable" by agents of the law.

So, too, are women of color specifically. Ironically, at the same time that women—and especially women of color—are under greater surveillance from a myriad of social institutions, they continue to be off the radar screen of largely white male police authorities. Increasingly, social welfare, educational, and health organizations penetrate and scrutinize the lives of poor women of color, seeking greater control over such areas as reproductive rights, and definitions of proper parenting (Bhattacharjee, 2002). Yet in another realm of the "private" sphere— woman abuse—police still fail to respond effectively in order to protect women of color (Bubar and Jumper Thurman, 2004; Deer, 2004). In fact, the interconnectedness of systems of social control is a significant deterrent to reporting violence. Victims are often fearful that their victimization may, ironically, result in having their children, rather than the offender, removed from the home. It signals a weakness on their part, that might be taken as a sign that they are unable to protect their children.

A rarely acknowledged though nonetheless important basis for the apparent failures of law enforcement to protect the rights of the Other can often be traced to the connection between state agencies and white supremacist organizations. The investigation that followed the taped beating of Rodney King revealed extensive organized white supremacist activity within the rolls of police agencies. The demographics and ideologies of police and white supremacist groups are strikingly similar. Both are predominantly white male institutions; both are committed to maintaining the established order. In short, the two entities share

> the "us" against "them" mentality which . . . makes the police susceptible
> to white supremacist preachings. The police . . . carry out a commitment to
> suppress threats to the hierarchy of the state and society which leaves
> Black people and other people of color at the bottom (Novick, 1995: 83).

Certainly the links are not as intimate or as extensive as in the past, when local sheriffs and their deputies were often Klan members. Nonetheless, monitoring organizations like the ADL and Southern Poverty Law Center's Klanwatch have documented a frightening tendency for white supremacist cells and individuals to once again emerge inside police departments. Moreover, these activists are doing more than spreading the message. They are acting out their ideologies in violent ways. They assault colleagues and citizens alike in their efforts to reconstruct a "white man's world," or as Omi and Winant (1994) put it, to re-articulate whiteness.

In its least extreme manifestation, the relationship between law enforcement and the white supremacist movement has been passive, in the sense that law enforcement officers fail to act against those organizations. In recent years, police complicity with white supremacist activities also takes the form of implicit or explicit support for Klan rallies and similar gatherings. This is manifest in a variety of ways: failure to police such rallies; off -duty police providing security for the rallies; police cordoning of

Klan parades and activities; and, at the extreme, the forcible suppression of anti-Klan demonstrators. Across the country, law enforcement agents have made their sympathies apparent by aiming their brutality at those resisting white supremacist activity. Given the tendency for the Klan or Aryan Nations rallies, for example, to lead to violence, this failure to prevent Klan activities is ultimately enabling. It clears the way for hate groups to engage in cross-burnings, harassment and assaults with little fear of police reprisals.

In sum, police activity and inactivity serve to marginalize communities of color. Racialized forms of policing constitute a climate which enables the simultaneous criminalization and victimization of people of color. The behaviors of police go as far to explain the over-representation of people of color in the justice system as do the behaviors of the individuals themselves. This chapter has provided broad outlines of these patterns across communities. The following chapters turn to the specificity of the historical and contemporary experiences of Native Americans in terms of both over- and under-policing.

Chapter 3
Colonial Policing and Beyond

The history of EuroAmerican victimization of Native peoples is as old as the history of EuroAmericans. Whether by violence or assimilationist policy, whites have consistently exerted their energies in the ongoing effort to physically or culturally annihilate Native peoples. Significantly the racialization of Native Americans has been invaluable to the processes of colonization. They are, in fact, inseparable, to the extent that the dehumanizing caricatures of Native Americans provided powerful rationales for colonial practices that denied the sovereignty of a people, as well as their related claims to their homelands. Racism—colonial racism to be more specific—is both a support for and an outcome of a legacy of colonization that has sought to eliminate the political, cultural, economic and territorial autonomy of Native Americans.

Colonial rule operated, in part, by constructing both discursive and institutional systems of difference and hierarchy. It thus required the "naturalization" of hierarchies, in this case, grounded in race, by which the colonized and colonizer could be distinguished. The related ordering process reinforced proscribed relations of inferiority and superiority. Colonial discourse thus racialized an autonomous people. Wherever possible, colonial authorities would respond to Native Americans not as a sovereign nation, but as inferior racial beings.

Specifically, colonial racism exploited the emerging science of race, i.e., social Darwinism, to reduce a diverse people to their racial features, relying heavily on racial imagery and emerging stereotypes to do so. This discourse of race—as created and reproduced by white Europeans—would define Native Americans as incapable of self-government, as childlike, uncivilized, or backward by turns. In so doing, the socially constructed hierarchies of race could be used to lend legitimacy to otherwise heinous practices of ethnocide and genocide. Moreover, social Darwinism would also provide the needed justification for "developing" the newly discovered land and its resources. Where the racialization of African Americans provided justification for their use as chattel, the racialization of Native Americans would allow unencumbered exploitation of their land and resources, as well as the denial of their nationhood. This is easily seen in the combined doctrines of Manifest Destiny and European superiority, providing as they did a clear rationale for genocide:

> When you set about to dispossess a people of their land and source of
> livelihood, unless you have no conscience at all, one must find an excuse
> to safely hide from the truth of the pain and suffering you are inflicting on
> innocent peoples. . . . If, indeed, these people (Native Americans) were
> human beings, then they were in fact a lesser type of humanity who had no
> rights to life, land or liberty. They could not use the land like Anglos, so
> they had no right to it; they had no civilizations, so they had no right to
> their own political institutions; their lives were not worth that of an Anglo,
> so they had no right to life (Jimson, 1992: 2).

From—or perhaps even before—first contact, the colonizers of what is
now North America saw themselves fully justified in laying claim to the
land and its resources. Under the related Doctrine of Discovery and the
principle of *terra nullus* the Spanish, French and English would variously
"occupy" the land and subjugate its people. No less an authority than John
Locke weighed in to support the Americans' claim to the Indian frontier. In
his *Two Treatises of Government* published in 1690, Locke offered his
assessment of the inability of Indians to properly "exploit" the rich land to
which they had laid claim. They were said to be

> rich in land and poor in all the comforts of life; whome nature having
> furnished as liberally as any other people with materials of plenty, i.e., a
> fruitful soil, apt to produce in abundance what might serve for good,
> raiment, and delight, yet for want of improving it by labor have no one-
> hundredth part of the conveniences we enjoy. And a king of large and
> fruitful territory there feeds, lodges, and is clad worse than a day-laborer in
> England.

This is an outstanding illustration of the ethnocentrism—and
paternalism—that underlie the rationale for overtaking the land so long
claimed by Indian nations. Rather than recognize that the indigenous
peoples preserved the land by taking only what was needed, Locke and his
colonial adherents disparaged them for their lazy and wasteful approach to
the land and its abundant resources. Dispossession, then, became a logical
imperative. The vast "wilderness" could best be tamed by those rugged,
self-sufficient, and hard-working Americans.

The colonization of the United States, then, like so many other similarly
affected sites, would revolve around the acquisition of land and its
resources. However, this would require the imposition of the will of the
conqueror over the will of the conquered. Thus, the historical patterns of
colonization experienced by American Indians have followed the typical
modes of conquest, including the diminution of Native control and
autonomy over their land base, through legal and extra-legal means. It
would also involve the suppression and destruction of native values and
ways of life by the colonizing power, resulting in the forced assimilation of
the colonized group into dominant society. The process is also associated
with the surveillance and regulation of the colonized by representatives of
the colonizers, as by armed forces or, more recently, by "Indian Affairs"
bureaucrats or law enforcement personnel. Moreover, the associated
practices of exploitation and oppression are justified by a colonizing and

racist discourse that insists upon the relative inferiority of the colonized people.

Colonial Policing: Dispossession and Assimilation

From the perspective of Europeans and Americans greedy for land and resources, policing the indigenous peoples who initially occupied the land became an integral strategy in the process of nation building. Law enforcement bodies—in varied guises—thus supported and often facilitated the colonialist project of the state. The social and legal order defended by police was also that of a colonial state, seeking to exclude or at least regulate native peoples who were seen to stand in the way of "progress." Specifically, law enforcement became the key means by which to "police" racialized spaces, and by which to facilitate the assimilative process.

In 1869, Indian agent Thomas Lightfoot proclaimed that "I have appointed a police, whose duty it is to inform me if they know if anything is wrong" (Parker, 1869). With this proclamation, Lightfoot announced the creation of the first formal Indian police force in Nebraska. This was a decidedly broad mandate, with an intended emphasis, no doubt, on anything that might be "wrong" with respect to Indians challenging their confining restrictions. But such an intervention also reflected a significant policy shift with respect to Native Americans "previously viewed (officially) as sovereign nations in charge of their own internal tribal affairs" (Peak, 1989). Lightfoot would use Indians to police their own community. Moreover, this was but one step in the dance that would see dramatic vacillation in terms of criminal justice policy in Indian country. Native sovereignty would by turns be contracted and expanded over time, with the net result of a significant loss of autonomy in decision making and control with respect to issues of crime (see table 3.1). This theme will be more fully articulated in a later discussion.

Table 3.1
Eras of Policing in Indian Country

Era	Dates	Characteristics
Traditional Policing	pre-1860	Clan specific; some warrior societies within clans
Reservation Police	1860-1880	Federal assertion of authority over reservations; development of bureaucratized tribal agencies; officers drawn from among tribal leaders
Federal Control of Indian Police	1880-1920	Centralization of Indian police; officers selected according to willingness to assimilate; seen as "agents of civilization"

Federalization of Indian Police	1920-1950	Extensive termination of federal relationship with tribes; Public Law 83-280 transferred responsibility for criminal law to specified states
Self-Determination	1960-present	Expansion of tribally controlled and funded police agencies

Adapted from Luna-Firebaugh, 2007.

There were facsimile predecessors to Lightfoot's tribal police force. However, these tended to have narrow, restricted duties. As early as 1795, a Cherokee tribal body was created to curb horse theft; in 1818, BIA agents were authorized by Congress to police trading with Eastern tribes; in 1830, the Indian Removal Act allowed for the use of the army as a national police force with the power to facilitate the forced relocation of resistant tribes; and in 1834, Congress expanded and combined the roles of the Bureau of Indian Affairs (BIA), U.S. Marshalls, and the army to create a "quasi-police" force (French, 2005; Harring, 1994). Later, following Lightfoot's lead, 130 Navajo and San Carlos Apaches were hired to act as a protective force for their respective reservations (1872). It is likely that the intent was as much to keep the Native Americans inside the boundaries as to keep any white threats out. In 1878, Congress authorized Indian police forces in Indian country, and by 1879, 800 Indians were on the payroll. However, it was after the Crow Dog case in 1881 that the creation of "real" police forces would begin apace.

The Crow Dog case on Lakota Sioux land would be a major turning point for native sovereignty with respect to policing at least. Crow Dog—a Lakota Sioux—shot and killed Spotted Tail, also a Lakota, but a tribal leader as well. He was tried, convicted and punished (by restitution) by the Sioux nation. However, he was later arrested and put on trial by American federal authorities. He appealed—and won—on the grounds that federal authorities lacked jurisdiction over crimes on Indian land. The decision sparked intense outrage in Washington over the spectacle of frontier lawlessness, and especially "uncivilized" tribal justice. For example, Secretary of the Interior Henry Teller, in advocating the Courts of Indian Offenses declaimed the state of affairs in Indian Country:

> Many of the agencies are without law of any kind, and the necessity for some rule of government on the reservations grows more and more apparent each day. If it is the purpose of the Government to civilize the Indians, they must be compelled to desist from the savage and barbarous practices that are calculated to continue them in savagery, no matter what exterior influences are brought to bear on them . . . (A) few non-progressive, degraded Indians are allowed to exhibit before the young and susceptible children all the debauchery, diabolism, and savagery of the worst of the Indian race. Every man familiar with Indian life will bear witness to the pernicious influence of these savage rites and heathenish customs (Teller, 1883: x).

To ensure the salvation of the "heathens," federal authorities proclaimed both the Courts of Indian Offenses (1883) and the attendant Major Crimes Act (1885). The latter extended federal jurisdiction for seven serious felonies committed on Indian land. This was the first official encroachment on tribal authority, which had heretofore been recognized as a condition and expression of sovereignty. Moreover, the threat would be exacerbated by the Dawes era allotment policies, which broke up traditional tribal land holdings into individual and family allotments. Curiously, the allotments were deemed to be under the jurisdiction of federal authorities. Thus, in the relevant parts of Indian Country, tribal authority over law enforcement was whittled away in piecemeal fashion. Moreover, this lessened the demand for Indian police per se. Slowly, they were replaced by "real" law enforcement bodies under the auspices of either local authorities or, increasingly, the BIA. The establishment of the Law and Order branch of the BIA buttressed the centralization and control of reservation police. By the mid-twentieth century, over 100 reservations had both BIA offices and BIA police agencies, with only the largest retaining tribal police (e.g., Navajo nation). In a later section, I will return to the theme of jurisdictional confusion and conflict.

In whatever guise, law enforcement bodies served two key colonial goals: dispossession and assimilation. The first of these strategies was carried out largely by military troops serving "police" functions. Cunneen (2001: 49-50) describes an official paramilitary police agency as a "force of dispossession." There was, however, no such parallel on the American frontier. Here it was left to the military to enforce colonial Indian policy.

Initially, it seemed as if the Native American population would represent a minimal obstacle to the conquest of the North American land base. They seemed easily overtaken, given the imbalance of fire power. Moreover, they proved fatally susceptible to common European diseases— small pox, measles, scarlet fever and venereal diseases, for example. It has been estimated that, between 1500 and 1900, Native Americans were subject to nearly 100 epidemics of European viruses (Stiffarm and Lane, 1992). Increasingly, these epidemics became part of the arsenal of Indian extermination. That infection was official policy is evident in the correspondence of British and American officers of the day. For example, Sir Jeffrey Amherst of the British forces assured a subordinate that "You would do well to (infect) the Indians by means of blankets as well as to try every other method that can served to extirpate this exorable race." Similarly, a captain in the U.S. forces wrote in a journal that "we gave them two blankets and a handkerchief out of the smallpox hospital. I hope it will have the desired effect" (cited in Stiffarm and Lane, 1992: 32). Native American vulnerability to disease was exacerbated by concerted efforts to deprive them of their traditional bases of nutrition, such as the destruction of their agricultural base, and the decimation of the buffalo population (Stannard, 1992). Ultimately, hundreds of thousands, if not millions, of Native Americans died of starvation, and in fact, whole nations were eliminated.

By the middle of the nineteenth century, Americans appeared to have lost patience with the slow pace of the epidemics in eliminating the "Native threat." Instead, they turned to explicitly genocidal policies and practices, and made no apologies for doing so. Policymakers spoke openly of the need to eliminate once and for all this troubling, savage people. In 1807, Thomas Jefferson insisted that "if ever we are constrained to lift the hatchet against any tribe, we will never lay it down until that tribe is exterminated, or is driven beyond the Mississippi . . . in war, they will kill some of us; we shall destroy all of them" (cited in Stannard, 1992: 120). Seven years later, Andrew Jackson, the noted "Indian-hater," would echo these sentiments: "I must distroy (sic) those deluded victims doomed to distruction (sic) by their own restless and savage conduct" (cited in Takaki, 1993: 85). And even later in 1882, a Philadelphia lawyer could still openly raise the same spectre: "We must either butcher them or civilize them, and what we do we must do quickly" (cited in Smith, 2005: 36).

Throughout the nineteenth century, military assaults on Indian villages became commonplace, especially where the residents had earlier refused to voluntarily give up their lands. Stannard (1992) claims that the intent was patently genocidal, insomuch as these villages were often occupied predominantly by women and children at times when the male population was away on hunting or fighting expeditions. As Stannard observes, a population deprived of its women and children cannot long survive. Among the most infamous of these assaults was the massacre of Sand Creek in 1984, where 105 Southern Cheyenne and Arapaho women and children and twenty-eight men were ruthlessly slaughtered by 700 heavily armed U.S. soldiers. In 1890, hundreds of Sioux were slaughtered at Wounded Knee, South Dakota. The tales of white savagery during this onslaught are legion. Those not killed by the powerful Hotchkiss cannons were hunted down and killed in their tracks, even women who bore flags of truce.

In all, these periodic forays accounted for tens of thousands of American Indian lives. Thousands more lives were lost in what policy makers of the day claimed as the more humane middle ground process of relocation. Those "fortunate" enough to be removed rather than executed nonetheless faced an equally grim fate, like the 8,000 Cherokee who perished on the 1,500 mile trek—at gunpoint—from their homeland in the east to Oklahoma. Along this Trail of Tears, nearly half of the original population was lost to exposure, malnutrition and exhaustion. Similarly, the Navajo's Long Walk and subsequent internment claimed 3,500 lives. It was to be the western military troops that would both oversee these marches, and the reservations that were their destination.

By the end of the nineteenth century however, Indian and BIA police had largely superseded the military, and thus mitigated the worst of the ravages associated with paramilitary control. This is not to say, though, that the effects were any less devastating. The transition to civilian policing represented a change of degree rather than of kind. I have argued elsewhere (Perry, 2002; Perry, forthcoming) that the history of North American colonialism can be traced through patterns of outright genocide, to more "subtle" forms of ethnocide. Policing in Indian Country was an integral arm of this trajectory, following a similar path from massacres to the repression of cultural traditions. In short, the law replaced the gun as an "agent of civilization" (Harring, 1994). Where the military had served its purpose in restricting the Native American land base, the police would serve to similarly restrict their cultural base. Increasingly, police became a key authority in the project of assimilation.

We saw in chapter 2 how one crucial dimension of policing generally is the regulation of race. This was certainly no less the case for Native Americans. Whether Indian police or municipal or other "white" police forces, they were tasked with the enforcement of a particular moral and social order that was at odds with the traditional indigenous order. Moreover, the imposition of Western legal ideals forcibly denied the legitimacy of traditional mechanisms of social control. Prior to, and later running parallel to, the imposition of Western legal traditions, Indian nations practiced their own social control traditions. Generally, these were grounded in distinct relations among and within families, clans, bands, and other recognized units. Formal law enforcement mechanisms often did not exist; rather, conflict resolution was grounded in informal decision-making within small collectives, whether clan or tribe. For example, the Cheyenne often organized camp soldiers to protect each encampment, maintained elaborate codes of justice, and saw tribal leaders as key authority figures in dispute resolution as in most other issues of import. Moreover, indigenous legal traditions reflected the particular economies and environments of particular nations. So, social control mechanisms of nomadic tribes like those in the central Plains were distinct from those of more place-bound communities as might be found in parts of the American Southwest. The establishment of Western legal principles in Indian country represented a direct threat to the sovereignty of Native peoples. It would purposefully whittle away at the traditions that had governed dispute resolution for generations. The Supreme Court, in *Montoya v. United States* in 1900 would explicitly, in fact, justify this intrusion, denying the ability of Native Americans to govern themselves:

> The North American Indians do not and never have constituted "nations" as that word is used by writers upon international law, although in a great number of treaties they are designated as "nations" as well as "tribes" . . . As they had no established laws, no recognized method of choosing their sovereigns by inheritance or election, no officer with defined powers, their governments in their original state were nothing more than a temporary submission to an intellectual or physical superior . . . In short, the word "nation" as applied to the uncivilized Indians is so much of a misnomer as to be little more that a compliment (US 261 (1900) at 265).

Such arrogant dismissal of what had heretofore been effective means of responding to conflict shows the absolute disregard that Americans had for Native life ways. Throughout the later part of the nineteenth century and early part of the twentieth century, such rhetoric paved the way for ongoing assaults on Native American sovereignty. Assimilation was seen as the answer to their "backwardness." They would be saved from themselves by opening their arms to embrace fully American ways. The goal, then, was to fully assimilate Native Americans into American culture, to encourage—in fact, coerce—them to leave behind their "heathen" and "uncivilized" ways. It is no surprise, then, that long lived traditions were supplanted by an alternative system meant to quash Native politics, economies, justice, religion and rituals. And the nascent frontier police forces were among the key architects of this new order.

At the outset, it is important to point out that the police did not assume sole responsibility for reforming the "savages." The race and place of Native Americans was defined and regulated by an array of intertwined formal and informal mechanisms of social control: missionaries, boarding schools, the military, even public health facilities. But increasingly these institutions would require the support and power of a formal police body:

> BIA schools could not function without compulsory attendance laws and BIA police to arrest or threaten parents for not sending children to school. BIA farmers could not teach the Indians to farm without laws and police to prevent Indians from killing their stock for food. Christian churches could not convert without laws to bar traditional ceremonial activities. Land could not be allotted without laws to punish Indians who resisted (Harring, 1994: 13).

Thus, police functioned explicitly to force the imposition of Western values and behaviors, and the suppression of traditional ways of living. They acted as "guardians" or administrators of the regulatory practices of containment and control (Cunneen, 2001). They would provide fundamental support for policies intended to outlaw Native traditions: religious rituals, long hair and braids, use of Native languages, and other related indicators of culture. For example, in 1897, the American government went so far as to call for military occupation of Zuni territory in an effort to forcibly halt traditional practices. In the closing years of the nineteenth century, police paid particular attention to cases of witch killings. In an 1887 case, the accused was to be transported to Northern Yakima territorial jail in broad daylight. The time of transfer was widely publicized so that it would draw an audience who would be witness to the "might and right" of white justice. In both cases, American frontier justice was meted out to Native Americans in a conscious and determined effort to enforce a peculiarly American social and legal order. Understandably, American-style law enforcement came to be seen as an invading force intent on cultural genocide (French, 2005; Harring, 1994; Million, 2000).

It was especially crucial for state agents to contain traditional religious practices in particular. The Americans were at least intelligent enough to know that in religion were to be found the foundations for a host of other societal norms. In the case of Native Americans, these norms were held to be a dangerous contrast to Western values, and thus a brake on assimilation. Consequently, law enforcement was tasked with containing practices such as traditional dances, and the use of peyote and other similar sacramental drugs. Interestingly, "where many immigrant and ethnic groups have found their traditional life patterns despised and ignored in the United States,

Indians are unique in that their traditions have been criminalized" (Bracey, 2006: 49). Indian police officers were especially reviled for their role in deculturating Indian nations. Even in appearance, they were blatant in eschewing the traditional trappings. They were required to emulate their white supervisors, by cutting their long hair, and dressing in "American" clothing. Yet they were also complicit in the destruction of tribal ways, tasked as they were with enforcing assimilationist policies. They could hardly be seen as other than traitors to their people, especially among those who had been forcibly removed to reservations due to their resistance against the "civilizing" forces of America. They were representatives of the oppressive state, and thus eschewed the importance of local and tribal traditions.

Resentment toward Indian police was evident in a number of ways. For one, community members were often unwilling to cooperate by providing information about "troublesome" activities or the whereabouts of Indians suspected of wrongdoing. At the extreme, such agents of the state might themselves become victims of violent crime in retaliation for their assumed role. Harring (1994) makes the claim that, while there were few intra-Indian killings through the nineteenth century, a fairly large proportion of those recorded are thought be murders of Indian police. This must have seemed fitting "justice" for those who

> became servants of the Great Father in Washington . . . Indian police officers not only gave up their braids and moccasins, but also campaigned against aspects of their own culture including ceremonial dancing, raiding for horses, and the influence of witches (Knepper and Puckett, 1995: 15).

Here is the extreme case of the double marginality (discussed at length in chapter 7) of police officers. In this case, the strongest resentment seemed to come from the community more so than from white authorities. They, in contrast, were quite happy to recruit those "progressives" who were willing to forego traditional life ways for the trappings of "power" in the white man's society. Washburn (1971: 171) makes the argument that this represented a way for Native American men to regain their warrior status, to regain "something he thought he had lost forever."

However, the recruitment of law enforcement agents from within the tribes was in no way intended to "give back" anything. On the contrary, it was intended to reinforce the imposition of western jurisprudence over Native American values and strategies of social control, that is, to render social control more effective through the employment of "insiders" who knew intimately both the people and their life ways. It was not a mechanism for making law enforcement more responsive to specific communities, but for making law enforcement appear legitimate by allowing Native Americans to ostensibly police themselves.

Sovereignty and Jurisdictional Confusion

The presence of tribal police was characteristic of the overlap of police agencies and jurisdictions that continues to represent the jurisdictional quagmire that is at the heart of contemporary conflicts around policing in Indian Country. Moreover, each historical expansion and contraction of federal, state or local jurisdiction in Indian Country must be seen as part of the historical intent to weaken Indian security and sovereignty.

Harring (1994) carefully analyzes four different conditions characterizing federal Indian policy in Indian country, some of which were in fact coterminous. Each illustrates a different level of tribal autonomy, thereby complicating the history of federal-tribal relations. The Corn Tassel case (Georgia, 1830) allowed state defiance of federal law and federal jurisdiction over Indian affairs. In the last half of the twentieth century, Indian Territory (modern day Oklahoma) enjoyed virtually unfettered tribal administration of justice. Of course, all of that would end when Oklahoma became a state in 1898. Crow Dog—discussed above—provoked the Major Crimes Act (1885), which would limit tribal authority with respect to specified serious crimes, thereby representing federal incursion on tribal autonomy. And finally, in Alaska, the prevailing model virtually extinguished tribal sovereignty, placing Native Alaskans under the full authority of state law.

The first thing to keep in mind is that law enforcement in Indian Country is in the hands of at least three levels of government: federal, state, and tribal (see table 3.2). In some cases, surrounding municipal police forces may also come into play. Jurisdiction may be partial, total, or absent, or even shared, and is defined by the combination of three deciding factors: location of the crime, nature of the crime, and race of victims and offenders. First, only crimes committed in Indian Country are under the jurisdiction of the tribes. All those outside these spaces—regardless of actors—are the purview of the federal or state police. Second, tribal jurisdiction requires that the offender must be Native American. They have no authority to intervene where the perpetrator is non-Native—a principle that was reinforced by the *Oliphant* decision. Finally, pursuant to the Major Crimes Act, tribes have authority only for relatively less serious crimes, leaving serious crimes—such as murder, manslaughter and arson—up to the federal agencies.

Table 3.2
State-by-State Overview of PL280

	Indian Country Affected
Mandatory States	
Alaska	All Indian Country except Metlakatla Indians of Annette Islands
California	All Indian Country
Minnesota	All Indian Country except Red Lake Reservation
Nebraska	All Indian Country
Oregon	All Indian Country except Warm Springs Reservation
Wisconsin	All Indian Country
Option States	
Arizona	Air and water pollution
Florida	All Indian Country
Idaho	State jurisdiction in seven areas if tribes consent: compulsory school attendance; juvenile delinquency and youth rehabilitation; dependent, neglected and abused children; insanities and mental illness; public assistance; domestic relations; motor vehicle operation
Iowa	Civil jurisdiction over Sac and Fox Reservation
Montana	Criminal jurisdiction over Flathead Reservation. State jurisdiction where tribes request, counties consent, and governor proclaims
Nevada	State jurisdiction, but counties may opt out; later amendment required tribal consent
North Dakota	Civil state jurisdiction only, subject to tribal consent
South Dakota	Criminal and civil matters arising on highways. State jurisdiction if United States reimburses costs of enforcement
Utah	State jurisdiction if tribes consent
Washington	Eight substantive areas of jurisdiction on Indian trust land; state jurisdiction over non-Indians and Indians on non-trust land, although state has allowed extensive retrocession

Adapted from Luna-Firebaugh, 2007: p 82

Parallel to this is the fact of different police bodies, with different affiliations. A lingering element of the colonial policing strategies is the presence of BIA police agencies on 64 reservations. These agencies are accountable only to the BIA and not at all to the tribes that they control. It is something of an understatement to say that BIA police "have an image problem, given that not so long ago their mandate was to keep tribal members confined to the reservation, to forcibly remove children from their homes and place them in boarding schools, to ration food, and to support the policies of resident agents of the U.S. government" (French, 2003: 78).

Ninety tribes provide law enforcement services under contract and funding from the BIA (see table 3.3). Given that they are ultimately accountable to the BIA, they have limited autonomy. In contrast, are those forces that are tribally funded—approximately 170 at present. These are accountable only to the tribes, with no ties of funding or protocol to federal or state governments. Not surprisingly, these departments tend to vary significantly in terms of operating standards and effectiveness. Additionally, twenty-five tribes have significant autonomy over law enforcement functions within their reservations, yet are funded by the Secretary of the Interior. And finally are those parts of Indian Country that have no local law enforcement program, and are instead policed by state and local authorities (Luna, 1998). One might add to the mix shared jurisdiction, where law enforcement agents from outside Indian territory are cross-deputized so as to extend their reach. The opposite is also common, that is cross-deputization of tribal officers so that they have some authority in geographically contiguous areas.

Table 3.3
Types of Indian Police Departments and Their Characteristics

	Public Law 93-638	BIA	Self-Governance	Tribally Funded	Public Law 83-280
Number	88	64	22	4	—
Trend	Increasing	Reducing	None	None	None
Administering Entity	Tribe	U.S. Government (BIA)	Tribe	Tribe	State/Local Law Enforcement Agencies
Entity Employing Officers	Tribe	U.S. Government	Tribe	Tribe	State/Local Law Enforcement Agencies
Funding	Federal - often with tribal contribution	U.S. Government	Tribe	Tribe	Primarily state/local entities

From Luna-Firebaugh, 2007: p 48

It is complicated enough to sort out what level of law enforcement prevails on a given reservation. This patchwork is made even more puzzling by the legal framework that qualifies the jurisdictional powers that inhere. First and foremost among these is the Major Crimes Act of 1885. Described above, this statute represents a significant incursion on tribal authority over serious crime, leaving seven criminal offenses to the jurisdiction of the federal government. The intimation is, of course, that Native Americans are incapable of investigating and prosecuting these on their own. The reality has been that the presence of the FBI on tribal land has not been welcomed by tribal members. Tony Hillerman's fictional characterization of the prickly relationship between local and federal authorities is, in fact, grounded in fact. During the era of termination, states would also be allowed to flex their law enforcement muscle in Indian Country through the enactment of Public Law 280 (1953). This act extended state authority over offenses committed against or by Native Americans in Indian Country in the specified states (California, Minnesota, Nebraska, Oregon, Wisconsin, and later, Alaska). Ten additional states opted for state jurisdiction over limited issues. Until 1968, no tribal consent was required for this usurpation of control; since 1968, no tribe has offered such consent. Nonetheless, the relevant states retain jurisdiction, to the detriment of tribal autonomy.

Public Law 93-638 of 1975 (also known as the Indian Self-Determination and Education Assistance Act) was an apparent effort to again shift the balance in favor of tribal autonomy. Section 101(d) observed that "subjecting Indians and Indian country to State or Federal civil and criminal law without regard to the unique cultural, political, geographic, and social factors of each Indian tribe and reservation is unjust and unworkable." Consequently, the statute enabled tribes to resume control over tribal law enforcement. They would remain funded by the BIA, would have the autonomy to determine the operational strategies for their communities. In theory, it seemed a good idea. It would allow unique nations to develop similarly unique responses to crime based on the needs of the local community. In practice, however, insufficient planning and training have left many such police forces with limited ability to effectively intervene in crime related problems (Wakeling, et al., 2001).

Ironically, Public Law 93-638 was enacted just three years before the *Oliphant* decision would cast a different light again on Native sovereignty. The 1978 decision renders Native American victimization at the hands of non-Natives jurisdictionally problematic, while at the same time also representing a lasting challenge to Native American self-governance. It revolved around the application of the Suquamish tribe's *Law and Order Code* to two cases involving white offenders. In a devastating decision, the Supreme Court ruled that tribal courts had no jurisdiction over non-Native offenders, thereby problematizing yet again the very question of Indian self-determination. The decision eroded tribes' abilities to police their own territory. It represented, to many Native Americans, yet another effort to redefine tribes not as sovereign nations, but as dependent states whose powers should be thus constrained.

The ongoing constraint of Native American sovereignty, according to Dian Million (2000: 102), is the

> founding narrative that naturalizes the American nation-state itself and its continuing hegemony over the country's land. *Jurisdiction*, a Western concept for the establishment of *law and order*, is at the heart of any modern practice of sovereignty. Native communities operate in mazes of law and policy well beyond those visited on other racialized peoples in the United States.

Moreover, it is the assertion of western values that has facilitated the criminalization of Native Americans. On the one hand, the strategies of colonization, containment and forced (albeit failed) assimilation have left Native Americans vulnerable to myriad social ills including substance abuse, property crime and violence. On the other hand, the colonial models of social control—including law enforcement—have themselves led to over-enforcement in Indian Country, so as to also "over-criminalize" Native Americans. It is to this that I now turn.

Chapter 4
Over-policing Native American Communities

The historical legacy of colonial policing, together with contemporary patterns of police activity draw us inexorably to one conclusion: that Native Americans are subject to disparate and discriminatory treatment at the hands of law enforcement. In the current era, policies like the much lauded "zero tolerance" approach has had dramatic implications for racialized minority groups generally, and Native Americans specifically. Communities frequented by Native Americans—whether urban or rural, on- or off-reservation—have been characterized by systematic harassment, and discriminatory, often brutal treatment of Native Americans. Policing is qualitatively, even quantitatively different in Native American communities. And given the preceding chapter, this comes as no surprise, for it is an extension of the colonial effort to regulate and marginalize indigenous people.

In the contemporary era, Native Americans have reason to believe that they are singled out, simultaneously for both undue attention and inattention. At one extreme is the "petit apartheid" of which Georges-Abeyie (1990) writes: the minor, ongoing, daily forms of harassment to which minorities—including Native Americans—are subject, the stop and search, the racial profiling, the racial epithets, the surveillance and suspicion, all of which are facts of life for many Native Americans. Neugebauer's (1999) and LaPrairie's (1994) interviews with Canadian First Nations people both reveal the extent to which indigenous people are treated with disrespect by police officers. Fully one-third of LaPrairie's respondents indicated that they received rude or verbally abusive treatment from police. Neugebauer's participants also indicated their perceptions that police officers commonly treat First Nations people with hostility, derision, and disrespect. One participant highlights: "the words of police officers. They commonly refer to us as 'savage,' 'squaw' or 'beast.' The white man has many terms to describe my people. Really, we get used to their nastiness. This abuse is actually quite common" (cited in Neugebauer, 1999: 252).

Moreover, the abuse is not only verbal. Physical abuse is also widespread. In 1994, in response to extensive complaints and media accounts of BIA officer brutality against Native Americans, the Committee on Natural Resources (Subcommittee on Indian Affairs) called a series of special hearings to explore the concerns. Participants from across the country testified to the history of brutality and the lack of response to the complaints lodged against officers involved. Helen Grace Blacklaw of the Wind River Indian Reservation observed that

> Police brutality is ignored here in the Wind River Indian Reservation. In the past, stories were heard of BIA police officers abusing people. Although it is hard to believe that such a crime exists in this day and age, police brutality is evident throughout the country, and is especially evident to us on the Wind River Indian Reservation (Committee on Natural Resources, 1995: 107).

Blacklaw's observations were reaffirmed by the testimony of Montana's Representative, Pat Williams: "excessive force, lack of due process, violations of civil rights, property damage are clear manifestations of a law enforcement system that is marked by lack of responsibility" (Committee on Natural Resources, 1995: 5).

It was with these images in mind that I included questions about law enforcement in my interviews. What was revealed was, in fact, consistent with the above. Many Native Americans feel that their communities are readily targeted by undue police attention:

> You file a complaint—it doesn't necessarily or usually get acted upon; a lot of times, they aren't. It is pretty rare that there was any satisfaction with the way things were handled. On the flop side, were you to do something—you better believe you know where you're going. They'll be right there on your tail. It's just a matter of how much you're gonna pay or how long you're gonna have to sit it out (Male, Montana).

This observation dramatically illustrates a pervasive theme in Indian Country: the over-enforcement of law against Native Americans. Heightened surveillance of Native American communities is an unavoidable outcome of perceptions of the community as inherently "troublesome" by virtue of their criminality, alcohol abuse, and lack of respect for American justice. The stereotypical belief in the deviance of Native Americans is used to justify what often appears as overreaction to the threat posed by this racialized group.

Across North America, it has long been the case that aboriginal communities—like many minority communities—are over-policed. Again, this is borne out by participants in my study. In the words of one,

> Law enforcement is "more thorough" with you. They ask more questions, spend more time. They just think you must have done something wrong. Even in a group of Indians and non-Indian, you will be grilled. A white guy will get a warning, an Indian will get interrogated or even charged with something minor. They're always looking for something to give you trouble for (Male, Montana).

This illustrates a key theme running throughout the interviews: that police appear to need little provocation to intervene *against* Native

Americans. To participants, officers appear eager to explore potential Native American wrong-doing in contrast to that of their non-Native counterparts. For example, "When white people get killed everybody wants to know who, and to catch 'em, especially if they think it was an Indian. But not when an Indian gets *killed*." It is as if police are ready and willing to accept the mythology of the "savage" Indian, and act accordingly.

Ultimately, in this process of over-enforcement, "police transform situational identities: victims are treated as suspects, and suspects as convicted criminals" (Neugebauer, 1999: 256). As an earlier comment suggested, police will find "something to give you trouble for." Moreover, as noted previously, this tendency is tied to the construction of cultural images:

> But that happens a lot with law enforcement; there's a lot of prejudice going around, there is, and with violence. There's just some examples that, you know, students would be doing something and they just assume just because they're Native American that they did something and they just put the blame on Native Americans and say "well, you did it, or something else at least." For an example, one of my relatives was going to school and the policeman went up there and checked him out and took him to the police station, they didn't even notify the parents, and said "well, just because he was hanging around with this group of kids." But that day, for some reason he wasn't; they just assumed that he was part of it, and they wanted to question him, they brought him down for questioning. . . . So, I mean, there's a lot of that going on all the time in town (Female, New Mexico).

Police action, then, is grounded in the pathologizing stereotypes that see Native Americans as inherently problematic—they are alcoholics; they can't be trusted; they are prone to criminality.

Policing the Mythical Indian

Police represent the frontline troops in the effort to maintain the place of racial minorities. As such, they carry into their interactions with Native Americans the same stockpile of stereotypes and images that shape the broader patterns of cultural imperialism. Neugebauer (2000: 87) argues that police use racial identity as a resource, to the extent that they "generalize situations in terms of fixed racist stereotypes located in both the occupational and the popular culture."

Underlying the stigmatization of Native Americans is a cluster of stereotypes that generally paint Native Americans as morally and intellectually inferior. Elevated rates of school drop-out, substance abuse, and unemployment are seen as causes rather than effects of their marginalized status. An apt illustration:

> 'Well, they can't handle that job, they're lousy drivers, they can't handle the job, they're lazy, they're drunks, they. . . . Oh, I remember a Christian in the Assembly of God Church, that said, because they sleep in a Hogan,

and the children get to watch their behavior, that they shouldn't be allowed to come to the Sunday school and be part of that group (Arizona, female).

As in this case, Native Americans feel that they are blamed and in fact ostracized for their own social problems, which are deemed to be rooted in their very natures. This occludes the structural mechanisms that leave far too many urban and rural American Indians on the fringes of society. Consequently, media, politicians, and popular discourse perpetuate the myths that portray Native Americans as morally bankrupt, lazy, even deceitful alcoholics. Moreover, as is typical of stereotypes in general, this image in particular is relatively immutable, even in the face of counter-evidence, something noted by the following participant:

> It's the way stereotypes are. People that have 'em, I mean, you could line you and I up and all of our students in a line and ah, and sober and motivated and educated and all that, and ah, you could have line up in a row, successful men, you could have one Indian walk by and is staggering with long hair, and they say now that's an Indian. And that's the perception, you know? It just hangs on and hangs on because stereotypes are like that (Minnesota, female).

Such pejorative stereotypes "promote injustice, disrespect, oppression, unequal treatment, and genocide. They keep people from understanding differences, similarities, problems and potential solutions" (Riding In, 2002: 25). In short, contemporary images of Native Americans continue to provide a rationale for both historical and contemporary practices that stigmatize and exclude them.

In her recent book on interracial relationships, Joane Nagel (2003: 55) makes the academic argument that "negative images or accusations about ethnic Others contribute to the creation of disreputable and toxic outgroups and can be used to justify their exclusion, repression, or extermination." In equally eloquent terms, a young man from Montana demonstrates just how the "toxic" images of which I've written here continue to impact the real lives of American Indians:

> And the hatred and the violence and the hurt, it's all mixed up in ideas of how Indian people are perceived, that they're savages, they don't know how to control themselves, or that they're violent. And in actuality, from history, it was the pioneers who were those things, not the Indians, not the Crow people. But that's continued, that attitude has continued, that native people don't know how to behave or follow the rules, I mean from an Anglo perspective, and so then Anglos have this feeling they have the right to inflict violence without, you know, they just think they can do it (Montana, male).

Individuals enter each social interaction carrying with them the baggage that holds these stereotypical images, and police officers are certainly no exception to this pattern. Racist discourse provides "a reservoir of procedural norms that not only tacitly inform routine activity, but are also able to legitimate more purposive, explicitly racist practices" (Smith, 1989: 150). It is within the cultural realm that we find the justifications for inequities, and for differential policing, in fact. For these processes are predicated upon legitimating ideologies and images which mark the Other, and the boundaries between self and other, in such a way as to normalize the corresponding inequities.

Consequently, the discriminatory practices that follow are in large part an outcome of negative stereotypes retained by law enforcement. So, it was not uncommon for participants to report the "usual" name-calling and racial slurs, as police officers referred to them as "Red," "Chief," or "Squaw." Moreover, participants shared the perception that police tended to fall back on that most persistent of and long-lived image of the "drunken Indian." Many shared the following sort of observation:

> Oh, people are targets. Uh, it's expected when you're driving and if you're having a few problems on the road, you'll get stopped just because you're Native, your dark hair, your dark skin, and they're just assuming that you're drinking. It's assumed that you're drinking and driving. And I've know people that have gotten over—I've been pulled over—because that was assumed. So that policeman comes around and says, well, the numbers show it, statistics say, study shows . . . self-fulfilling prophecy (Male, Arizona).

> I think the reason that it comes up though, is because—we were talking about racism in relation to law enforcement—and I think that alcohol is a real easy peg to hang, I mean, that's the first thing that triggers most acts of law enforcement around here to begin with. It's the alcohol and traffic stuff. I mean, the rationale for the road blocks and stuff is, even to catch people who aren't drunk with other kinds of violations, is because they're set up to catch people who are driving while drunk, so that's where it sort of starts (Female, Wisconsin).

Where youth are involved, the labeling takes a slightly different tone, mirroring the more general tendency to presume gang affiliation among young men of color. One educator, referring to young Native American men observed that "the police follow them, thinking they are always up to no good or in gangs." A youth, with a circle of peers nodding their heads in agreement, claimed that "if they see a bunch of us together, they think we're in a gang or doing drugs or getting ready to do something wrong. They don't treat us right." In short, participants suspected that police were always ready to think the worst of them, to diminish their worth by reverting to gross and inaccurate generalizations of American Indians.

Moreover, it was not just potential suspects who garnered negative assessments on the part of police. Victims, too, are often viewed through the same uncomplimentary lens. One officer, in fact, turned the "drunken Indian" stereotype into a neat excuse for the racial violence:

> When I first started working down here, they all commented— "Farmington? I can't believe you got on in Farmington. Why do you want to go there? They don't like Indians!" And it's like, no, I don't see it that way. We have a lot of downtown drunks, homeless people, not only Native American, but mostly. And they just get the trouble they get just because

they're homeless, just because they're drunk. It's never a racial thing, or once in a while. It's just stupid comments. But in the three or four years I've been here, I don't recall any racial violence as such (Female, New Mexico).

Like the broader population, law enforcement too is prone to falling back on historical images to excuse their own discriminatory treatment of Native Americans. Moreover, their images of the appropriate "place" of Native Americans also informs their treatment of them, as the next section argues.

Profiling and the Racialization of Space

Few contemporary practices can so effectively serve to put Indians "in their place"—and keep them there—as racial profiling. It demonstrates for its subjects—as if they didn't know already—the spatial and cultural boundaries beyond which they must not travel. This was broadly perceived by study participants to be a particularly widespread problem; few practices were seen to be as pervasive.

Throughout the history of the United States, whiteness has been conceived as the norm, thus supporting racialized boundaries which assume whiteness as the standard against which all others are judged. It divides white from non-white, "unraced" from "raced." There is an ideological presumption of innate, biological differences between races which is then extrapolated to cultural and ethical differences. One's biological race is understood to determine one's "essence," to the extent that physical characteristics are linked to all other elements of one's identity. This construction of racial difference subsequently justifies the full array of practices associated with racial exclusion and marginalization. Since difference has been understood negatively in the United States, it has come to signify deficiency or deviance. Consequently, "non-white" is equivalent to difference and inferiority. "Non-white" is the antithesis of white, and must necessarily remain subordinate to white. Moreover, "(w)hiteness is generally (and paradoxically) defined more precisely by who is excluded than who is included. Whites are those who are not nonwhite, those who are not racially marked, those who are not clustered together to form a category or racial minority" (Blee 2004: 52).

As this suggests, race also implies "insides" and "outsides," places of belonging and not-belonging, such that certain people may be seen to be in or out of "their places." Such race-based juxtapositions are central to legitimating and rationalizing the marginalization of the Other who stands outside the boundaries of whiteness: "The ability to create and enforce these boundaries is related to societal power, as different formations of power rely on territorial rules about 'what is in or out of place' for their existence" (Sumartojo, 2004: 89). Our "place" thus becomes racialized, thereby shaping our lived experiences and related life chances. The connection between race and place is much more than a merely symbolic metaphor. It has dramatic material consequences as well. Consider Razack's assessment:

> When police drop Aboriginal people outside the town limits leaving them to freeze to death, or stop young Black men on the streets or in malls, when the eyes of shop clerks follow bodies of colour, presuming them to be illicit, when workplaces remain relentlessly white in the better paid jobs and fully "coloured" at the lower levels, when affluent areas of the city are all white and poorer areas are mostly of colour, we experience the spatiality of the racial order in which we live (Razack, 2002: 6).

This talk about inside and outside, about border crossing, and other spatial metaphors implies the centrality of geographical understandings of racial formations. In short,

> Geography is relevant to the social construction of race and ethnicity because identities are created not only by the labels that are borne but through the spaces and places within which they exist . . . geography, the spaces and places that we exist in and create simultaneously shapes and records the way life unfolds, including the lived experience of ethnicity and race (Berry and Henderson 2002: 6).

As the preceding implies, central to our understanding of the geography of race is one particular element of the spatial as it relates to racial construction: boundaries, or borders. Borders are especially important as markers of the distinct boundedness of racialized groups, setting the limits as to who belongs where. They symbolically (and often physically) determine and reinforce ethnic separation and segregation. Whiteness, in particular, is a closely guarded fortress which is, by and large

> defined by its boundaries . . . In determining whiteness, borders are more significant then internal commonality. Over time whiteness has been constructed, in the words of the legal theorist Cheryl Harris, as "an exclusive club whose membership was closely and grudgingly guarded" (Blee, 2004: 52).

Significantly, boundaries signify both the social and spatial margins of race. They can take the symbolic form of cultural difference, of legislative control, or popular imaging. Yet they are likely to assume a spatial dimension, such as walls, fences, or railroad tracks. Native American reservation boundaries, for example, represent something in between. They are invisible geopolitical borders, which nonetheless assume—in the imaginations of both Native and non-Native—a very real presence and impediment between residents and non-residents (Sumartojo 2004).

Consequently, racial profiling of Native Americans in and around reservations becomes an important means by which to reinforce historically conditioned patterns of segregation. This was disturbingly evident in the words of this participant:

> I've seen them just sit there by that bridge—that's the border—and they'll

sit here all day and just keep stopping us when we have tribal plates. It's
like, as soon as we leave the res, we're stopped for any or no reason. It
makes you not wanna leave, you know (Male, Montana)?

This was an especially striking example, illustrating the sanctity of the
reservation boundary. However, it was by no means an anomalous incident.
From the perspective of many Native Americans, it appears to be a daily
reality, especially in border communities where cultural boundaries are
reinforced by geographical ones:

> I think that profiling came early on with our plates here at White Earth . . .
> You see people stopped all the time. I've been driving back and forth
> between Cass Lake and here and Red Lake, and ah, I see people stopped
> all the time. There's a lot of harassing done by the police when they stop
> Indians with reservation plates (Female, Minnesota).

As the last example suggests, once stopped, Native Americans are
potentially subject to additional layers of disrespect, hostility, occasionally
violence. An example at the lower extreme:

> I know, some people that I know, come into town and leave town, usually
> they're stopped for something, and the cop really doesn't say for sure why
> they're stopping this driver. They've just been stopped, and there's no law
> that says, hey, this is the reason why I stopped you, but I found something
> else. There's a lot of that . . . And don't ever question them, or ask why
> you were stopped. That really pisses 'em off, so they'll throw more
> charges at you; they just get mean and rude, call you names they shouldn't
> (Male, Montana).

Selective attention creates a vicious self-fulfilling prophecy. Almost
inevitably, the undue attention paid to Native Americans deemed to be
outside of their proscribed places means that they run a heightened risk of
criminalization. Elevated surveillance of Indian communities results in
higher rates of crime detection and charging. The elevated crime rates will
draw more attention to these "crime prone" areas, which will again lead to
inflated rates of detection and arrest. Moreover, the problem is exacerbated
by a parallel tendency to over-charge Native suspects.

Many participants told tales of police "inventing" charges, especially in
the face of confrontational Native Americans. One participant described
how a police officer invoked a litany of racial slurs in response to her
challenging a speeding ticket—which was ultimately raised rather than
lowered. The following story highlights more concretely the ironic turns
police activity can take.

> It's funny you're here today. I'm still shaking—last night was really bad.
> The cops just want to give us a bad time here; they gotta find something
> once they start looking. He comes, the cop comes to my door after I got
> home, says he's comin' in, says he knows there's things, stolen stuff there,
> that my son took some stereos and videos and stuff from some peoples'
> houses. I say no way, but they came and looked. Of course, there wasn't

nothing, no stuff for them to find. I still don't know why they came looking. But next thing I know, there's more people at my door—social services. They took my little girl, they made her go with them and she's crying and I'm crying and screaming at them. I guess, they were pissed they couldn't find no stuff or something. They called services and told them my kids were living in a hell hole, that it was filthy and the kids could be sick. So the social service people, they came over and said, yeah, kids can't live like this and take my little girl! I called Bob, and he went over, said they have no right, etc. It took 'til this morning before I came to work to make them let me have my girl. That's what happens here; they gotta find something. And if there isn't, if they're wrong, they'll make something up. Why would they say my house isn't safe? Sure, I don't clean every day, but I'm trying to do all this myself. They get food and baths and clean clothes. I can't afford no maid like they think I should or something. Cops got no right to judge me 'cause I'm too busy to mop the floor (Female, Wisconsin).

This case is especially educative, revealing disturbing tendencies: the tendency to "create" suspect conditions; and second, the enforcement of white middle class definitions of child welfare. Ultimately, such interactions leave a legacy of fear and distrust. The lesson learned is "don't ever question them, or ask why you were stopped. That really pisses 'em off, so they'll throw more charges at you; they just get mean and rude, call you names they shouldn't." And not only do they "call you names." The police response to perceived challenges to their authority can escalate to violence.

Police Violence

Law enforcement officers frequently step over the boundaries of "legitimate" force to engage in the illegitimate and excessive use of force. Recent years have called attention to this tendency, especially through the highly publicized cases such as Rodney King, Abner Louima, and Amadou Diallou. These cases also highlight the fact that people of color are dramatically over-represented as victims of police violence (Cole, 1999; Russell-Brown, 2004). Equally important, however, is the recognition that popular attention to these celebrated cases obscures the mundane, routine instances of police harassment and abuse of people of color.

In chapter 2, I referred to the Mollen Commission, reporting in 1994. Officers openly admitted to the Commission the widespread use of brutality and violence, especially against members of racialized communities. In revealing testimony one officer admitted that it was not simply suspects that suffered this fate; rather, "we just beat people up in general. If they're on the street, hanging around drug locations. Just—it was a show of force;" he added that the purpose was "to show who was in charge. We were in charge, the police" (Mollen Commission, 1994: 27).

Such sentiments clearly reveal the role that violence—alongside the profiling noted above—plays in policing race and space. It is an integral strategy in the reaffirmation of the line between "us" and "them." Like profiling—but more forcefully—police use of violence is a means of keeping racial minorities in their place. It is a reassertion of social and geographical space that is to be occupied by the targets. It thus becomes a territorial defense of cultural "space." It is a means to reassert the marginality of the other who dares to transgress. Like the hate crime perpetrated by civilians, the racialized violence exercised by police

> are exclusionary acts motivated in part by offenders' desires to assert power over a given space, whether it be a neighborhood or public street. The effect of such acts is to send a "message" to members of the targeted group that they are unwelcome. In addition, hate crimes and responses to them contribute to the meaning of a place, representing a struggle between the meanings informing offenders and those informing other groups (Sumartojo, 2004: 105).

In light of this, then, it is perhaps not surprising that Native Americans shared their observation that, upon stopping Native American drivers or pedestrians, police officers were not above the use of violence themselves. It is, of course, a truism that police hold a monopoly on the legitimate use of force. However, when dealing with people of color and with indigenous people, they are not above responding with what is perceived to be the illegitimate and excessive use of force.

This appeared to be particularly the case of youth, who were most likely to share their own experiences of overly zealous stop and search practices, for example:

> We hate the cops 'cause they hate us. If they see a bunch of us together, they think the worst, they think we're in a gang or doing drugs or getting ready to do something wrong. They don't treat us right. Me, us—a lot of us—the cops give us a real hard time, like they're the boss. They'll stop us and ask us what we're doing, where we're going. They don't believe us anyway (male, New Mexico).

Away from the gaze of the public eye, police are able to shift their methods of control and restraint, to become less circumspect in their behavior. Neugebauer (2000: 92) observes the ways in which officers direct the "rhythm of exchange" between themselves and those they may load into their cruisers, such that power is maintained through a combination of "exaggerated displays of legal power and physical prowess."

> One time—that time you know?—me and them two were going to play pool, but they stopped and gave us trouble, told us to get in the car. They started driving us around—man, this is Farmington, that scared us. But they drove behind the school and made us get out then started hitting on us, and kicking us. No one to tell—'cause they're the cops. I know other guys got, did, they did this to them too. It's a lot of us here, 'cause the cops think they need to give us shit just in case we did something they don't know about—like all we wanna do is steal, or smoke drugs (Male, New Mexico).

One participant related an incident she observed at a local grocery store. This example highlights the potential for violence when police confront Native American "suspects:"

> One time I went to Safeway, and there's this lady, she was standing in line over there and the police, I guess somebody called, I don't know who called. She was standing around, bothering nobody, standing on the side of the phone booth, and here comes a cop; he stopped right there, and he grabbed the lady by the arm and pulled her over to the police car, and there was a little gap, I guess where the curb was right there, and somehow he pulled her over, we were just watching. I don't know how old she was, about forty to fifty, and she was kinda feeling good, minding her own business there, and here comes the police, grabs her, yanks her by the police ride, and I guess she didn't see the step down, maybe six inches, she almost fell. And the police grabs her back up and kind of twists her, and she was hurting, she was kind of crying, and he starts yelling at her. They figured, "drunk as a trunk, we don't care" and that's how they treated her. No respect for her, no trying to make sure she's not hurt (Female, New Mexico).

As noted earlier, challenges to the authority of police are especially likely to elicit a hostile, even violent response, as the following examples illustrate:

> And then, even yesterday, there were these two guys, just by the phone booth between Styx and Taco Bell, something, they were hanging around there, and he was leaving the other guy drunk, and they kick him in the knee, and try to pull him in the police car. He wasn't fighting them. But people say something to police and then they go back and put all kinds of charges. Right away they said to him, "resistant to arrest, intoxicated in public, disorderly conduct," something, everything was on him right there. That's what happened, right in front of us too. So the other guy was just hanging around, "you're with him, you're in the same situation so get in the car." The more you say things, the more they add to the list. It is kind of like that here; they add more stuff on there than what it's supposed to be if you are a mouthy Indian (Female, New Mexico).

> Several incidents that's happened here, and another thing is that we were talking about the police. They would arrest you, and they won't just talk to you nice; they'll manhandle you, they'll kick you around, and I was coming down about two years ago, I saw a car, I could see the lights around the corner. I saw the flashing lights and I got out and there were five squad cars and that car and they had him sprawled out on top of the hood, sprawled out like that. It was dark, but I'd swear he was all bloody. So I pulled up and said "is there anything I can do here?" "Okay smart-alec, keep on going." I kind of looked to see who he was, he said, "Did you hear what I said there Red?" and he pushed me hard, out of the way, tried to spin me around; and they were not nice and that's the way they act down here, you know (Male, Minnesota)?

For the respondent cited in the last example, such interactions with the police were a fact of life. This was a vocal community activist who says he often found himself at risk of police violence. He says "every time I go to a demonstration, or when I've had a letter in the paper, or sometimes I go to court to help a friend—every time they conveniently pull me over, rough me up a bit, and then drive off." The clear message here: mind your place! A much more dramatic case highlights the risk involved in confronting police. Another man active in the community shares this story:

> My co-worker, or counterpart . . . he filed a lawsuit in the U.S. district court and it was going to be heard, it was on a Monday, you know, that's when it was scheduled to go to court. Well, that Saturday night, the same sheriff's deputy that was doing this stuff to these women out in Mayawash, pulled him over, and he had been drinking some, but pulled him over, impounded his car, took him home at like one thirty in the morning or something, and the next morning, when some other people stopped by they walked into his house, and there he was dead, and they looked at it and said, "oh suicide." But the last person to see him alive was this sheriff's deputy and you know, there was this court thing that was going to engage that following Monday. What finally ended up happening, my co-worker, my friend, he's dead, and that's how they left it, "ah, he shot himself." The guy didn't own a gun, he was not a hunter, he was raised in the Twin Cities, but he wasn't raised on the reservation where all those skills evolved, he didn't own a gun, he wasn't a hunter type of a person, but . . . no investigation (Male, Wisconsin).

Ongoing, widespread brutality on the part of a single officer was at the heart of another story of police violence. A participant told the story of a police officer who had been coercing American Indian women to have sex with him, for example, by threatening to frame her boyfriend if she didn't comply. Moreover, the sexual assaults on these women were perceived to be part of a broader pattern of disrespect and violence against the entire community:

> When they ended up charging that sheriff's deputy, they charged him with a number of things. Here, they called it sexual misconduct, you know, first and second degree, sexual misconduct, which is rape, uh, and also using the, using excessive force under the authority of the law to do things like break up parties. I mean, he would go in and just start busting heads and breaking up a kid's party or something, you know, he'd trash the place, you know, night sticks, and boots and heels and this is how he'd break up a party, and um, you know, most times it was Indians at these parties, never hurting anybody or bothering anybody, but he'd go in and do it (Male, Wisconsin).

Reports of police misconduct toward Native Americans—running the continuum from negligence to extreme forms of violence—were consistent across the interviews, regardless of location. Like racial violence perpetrated by citizens, police mistreatment of American Indians appears embedded in both the broader culture and the police culture. In a nutshell, participants described at one and the same time both the over- and under-enforcement of their communities. On the one hand, should they somehow draw attention to themselves—often simply by appearing in public—they ran the risk of becoming the target of police harassment and violence; on the other hand, as the following chapter will demonstrate, their own complaints were perceived to be trivialized and/or ignored As one woman succinctly described the paradox:

> There's a lot of violence here, Indian on Indian, white on Indian, Indian on white. What makes it easy is the police are really bad. They don't do anything; worse, they beat Indians, especially young guys, real bad and follow them, thinking they are always up to no good or in gangs. They'll go out of their way to pick up Indians. They just get treated different (Female, Minnesota).

Jefferson (1994: 254) has made a similar observation with respect to the experiences of racial minorities in the UK, who have long seen police as "a hostile and alien force—one which has subjected their communities to aggressive, harassing, and intimidating "over-policing," yet has been only indifferent or half-hearted in the face of black and Asian victims of racist attacks." Like many other people of color, Native Americans may very well perceive themselves to be in need of protection from the police, rather than being able to rely on police to protect them. It is to the other side of this coin that I now turn.

Chapter 5
Under-policing in Native American Communities

Contrary to the universal police mantra "to serve and protect," many Native Americans perceive their communities to be underserved and unprotected. Ironically, while Native American communities may be disproportionately surveilled by police, this does not necessarily result in heightened protection. The surveillance is for the purposes of responding to Native American offenders, rather than Native American victims. Their communities are deemed worthy of regulation, but in the interests of state and hegemonically defined rules of order, not in the interests of the residents per se. This is a factor that has been sadly neglected in the literature on policing race generally, and policing Native Americans specifically. Yet it is typical enough to leave Native American communities vulnerable to an array of violations and indignities.

The policing literature is clear on the fact that virtually all racialized communities within the United States are subject to law enforcement's tendency to under-police—and thus under-protect—their communities (Black, 1980; Cunneen, 2001; Cook-Lynn, 2001). It is indisputable that this is a universal problem for non-whites across the country. Clearly, Native Americans are subject to the same lack of attention and urgency in response crime problems in their communities, whether rural or urban, on- or off-reservation. And this pattern is largely conditioned by myriad structures of systemic discrimination. However, Native American communities are disadvantaged by two relatively unique factors: jurisdictional issues; and staffing issues. Together, these structural realities of policing in Indian Country enable the non-responsiveness of law enforcement.

The jurisdictional complexity noted in chapter 3 lends itself to a failure to adequately protect Native Americans. This is a feature that plagues Native Americans alone, in that, in Indian Country "Native communities operate in a maze of law and policy well beyond that visited on other racialized people in the Unites States" (Million, 2000: 102). This allows crime in and around Indian country to fall through the cracks when there is any confusion as to who is intended to take the lead.

This is exacerbated by two related factors. First, there appears to be a tendency for federal officials to shirk their duties with respect to investigations and prosecutions in Indian Country (Deer, 2004). Limited protection can be offered when offenders are not pursued as forcefully as might be the case elsewhere.

The second related problem is the general understaffing of law enforcement agencies across Indian Country. This is very much in line with the broader pattern of inferior quality and quantity of public services available to Native American communities (Deer, 2000; Smith, 2005). Indeed, a federal committee found that "basic law enforcement protection and services are severely inadequate for most of Indian Country" (Executive Committee for Indian Law Enforcement Improvements, 1997). The same report firmly laid the blame for this lack of protection on the parallel lack of funding and resources. This is especially evident with respect to personnel, in that staffing ratios are dangerously low in Indian Country relative to national trends:

> One of the most telling indicators of inadequate law enforcement services in Indian Country is the chronic shortage of personnel. For example, the 1996 UCR statistics show 2.9 officers per 1,000 citizens in non-Indian communities under 10,000. The equivalent ratio in Indian Country is 1.3 officers per 1,000 citizens—less than one-half the per capita coverage in small communities outside of Indian Country. Approximately 1,600 BIA and tribal uniformed officers must patrol the 56 million acres of tribal lands in the lower 48 states. On the 17.5 million acres owned by the Navajo Nation, the ratio of officers to citizens is only 0.9 per 1,000. Remote areas, poor roads, and no backup not only result in poor service to the people, but also stressful and dangerous jobs for the officers (Executive Committee, 1997).

Yet it is not only these resource issues that come into play. In the preceding chapter, I referred to the ways in which popular constructions of "Indian-ness" informed their over-policing. The same might be said of under-policing. Those same racialized perceptions of Indian identity are often used to blame the victim so as to deny the significance—or even the reality—of their victimization.

Denial

It is a truism within criminology that, from a law enforcement perspective, there are "deserving" victims and "undeserving" victims. That is, there are those whose victimization can and should be taken seriously, and those whose parallel experiences should not. It would appear that Native Americans are thought to fall into the latter category. Somehow, injury, loss, or damage that affects them is less serious, and thus less worthy of either immediate or concentrated attention. So entrenched is the vision of Native Americans as criminals and/or alcoholics that law enforcement seems reluctant to acknowledge them as victims. They can be only one or the other from this perspective–either victims or offenders—and it is much more in line with the stereotypical Indian to see them as somehow at fault. Should they present themselves as victims, it can only be because they have somehow brought it upon themselves—they've provoked the victimization or deserved it by virtue of their drunkenness. At the risk of repetition, I cite here a police officer quoted in the previous chapter:

> We have a lot of downtown drunks, homeless people, not only Native American, but mostly. And they just get the trouble they get just because they're homeless, just because they're drunk. It's never a racial thing, or once in a while. It's just stupid comments. But in the three or four years I've been here, I don't recall any racial violence as such (Female, New Mexico).

This officer deftly sidesteps the culpability of the offender, instead "blaming the victims" for their own harm. Constructing Native Americans as "undeserving" victims limits the responsibility of law enforcement to seriously consider the possibility of harm. Police are able to invoke techniques of neutralization that diminish if not deny the danger faced by individuals or the community at large. Consequently, the putative offender is absolved of guilt, and law enforcement is absolved of the need to respond.

Equally common was the tendency for police to treat complainants as "just another Indian bitching about nothing." Police officers themselves provided evidence to support public assumptions. One officer affirmed this very fear, saying, "Everybody has to have a complaint about that, you know, because somebody's Native American or someone's minority, there's a complaint. You hear about it, but I wonder sometimes" (Male, Montana).

Another asserted his belief that Native Americans overplay the race card, and "use the notion of the 'White Man' as a political ploy." He went on to say that "Much of the distrust between communities is the fault of the Native people, who think everyone is racist and is discriminating. The Tribe brings stereotypes upon themselves, and use stereotypes." In short, these officers go beyond blaming the victim, to also deny the victim outright.

Recall the brief discussion of the distribution and frequency of victimization reported by participants across the country. That summary noted that it was a wide-ranging, normative fact of life for Native Americans living in and near reservations. How, then, to account for observations like the following made by police officers serving in reservation communities?

> Q. Do you think, you're saying that it is not as widespread?
> A. Most people feel safe and this is for the people here that are the tribal members here on the reservation and from what I see over the years. I've lived here and worked here or lived or outside the reservation, worked inside the reservation. The majority of people just want to get along. Go about their business, live their lives, don't want any problems and they won't do anything of a prejudiced nature of, that wouldn't be considered a hate crime because they wouldn't want to get involved in something like that. They're overall just good law-abiding citizens, there are just a few bad apples that love to instigate a little problem and looking for a scapegoat in life and it is always easy to blame one race no matter which race it is. Blaming another for some type of problem (Male, Wisconsin).

I think in the social aspect there's no conflict, no discrimination; there's
really nothing. Sometimes people will talk about it, but I don't think they,
uh, I think they often make it up. I don't see it, and nobody comes directly
to the station to complain. So, no, if they complain about it, I think they are
wrong (Male, Minnesota).

Such declarations fly in the face of the experiences described so
candidly by people in all of the communities visited. Such blindness—wilful
or otherwise—to the plight of the people they are intended to serve speaks
volumes about how police view Native American communities. Where there
is "no violence," there can be no reason for action:

You don't want to call the police or make an issue of it. They play down
how serious the violence is, how much there is—unless it's Indians hurting
whites. They see the cases one at a time if at all, so they won't make the
connections. The cases aren't related; it's not about discrimination, they
say. They won't admit that Indians get hurt more (Male, Montana).

Denial of the problem absolves them of the responsibility of
confronting it. Where victimization does not occur, where it is merely
"imagined" by "wannabe" victims, police can and do turn a blind eye to
violence perpetrated against Native Americans, as noted by Gordon (2000:
369):

The list of unsolved murders, along with the clear reluctance of victims
even to report (racist) incidents, must stand as a clear indictment. The
police, it is clear from numerous reports and studies over the years, have
with a remarkable consistency denied the racist nature of attacks, played
down the seriousness of attacks, often treated victims with hostility and
lack of sympathy, allowed alleged attackers to go free and, until recently,
refused to make use of their powers to prosecute alleged offenders except
in very serious assault cases.

This resonates with Cook-Lynn's (2001) observations about police
denial of victimization. She describes the response to the death of Many
Horses in Mobredge, SD in 1999. Many Horses was allegedly beaten by
four white youths, tossed into a garbage can and left to die. Police cited
Many Horses' alcoholism, not the youths' racism as the key contributing
factor: "those in charge of the law and legal services of this white
community would never allow this death to be called a killing or a murder,
let alone a hate crime. . . . It was not a hate crime, according to those who
investigated the event. It was not even a murder" (Cook-Lynn, 2001: 213).

Failure to Act

Inevitably, one of the consequences of denying the legitimacy or urgency of
Native American victimization is the resultant failure to act on the
complaint. This is one of the defining elements of under-policing racialized
communities, and is often justified on the basis of the jurisdictional

quagmire noted above. That is, the difficulties of investigating anti-Indian violence are exacerbated by long term structural problems. Most notable is the message sent by the Supreme Court in the 1978 *Oliphant* decision. It revolved around the application of the Suquamish tribe's *Law and Order Code* to two cases involving white offenders. In a devastating decision, the Supreme Court ruled that tribal courts had no jurisdiction over non-Native offenders. In the context of victimization, the decision would seem to imply that Native Americans have little legal recourse to protect themselves from white offenders. State, or more likely federal, authorities could, of course, be called in. However, given the relatively minor nature of most racially motivated incidents, the state and the FBI have limited interest in pursuing such cases. Moreover, as noted above, the staffing levels often prohibit such investigations.

Other factors play a role in the failure of police to intervene. Indeed, if police violence represents an explicit violation of Native American rights, failure to respond effectively to Native American victimization is a more "subtle" implicit violation. It represents a failure to protect victims from violence inflicted by others. It suggests that Native Americans are less worthy of the protection afforded their white counterparts. Moreover, it lends permission to offenders, to the extent that such apathy leaves perpetrators unpunished. This is tantamount, in fact, to condoning Native American victimization. It says to the offender—and those who might next victimize Native Americans—that there will be no serious repercussions for their crimes.

It is not uncommon for police to respond ineffectively to what might be understood as hate crimes—those motivated by racial animus. There is a small but growing body of scholarship that has begun to explore this very issue (Parker, forthcoming). Most striking, perhaps, is the apparent divide between victim's perceptions of hate crime, and subsequent.police determinations of hate crime. Comparing victim reported statistics in BJS data to police recorded statistics in FBI date, Parker (forthcoming) observes that "the gulf between the 191,000 *perceived-by-victim* hate crimes and a maximum of 9,730 *confirmed-by-police* hate crimes raises the question of whether the inconsistency can be attributed largely to victim misperception or instead attributed to law enforcement failures." Additionally, consider the data presented in table 5.1, comparing hate crime recorded by two different advocacy organizations and in the FBI Uniform Crime Report. Granted, advocacy organizations' data gathering techniques are non-systematic, and include incidents that do not legally constitute crimes. Nonetheless, the gap between the various data sets is remarkable.

Table 5.1

Sample Comparisons of UCR Hate Crime Data to those Collected by Anti-Violence Organizations

| | Anti-Semitic | | Anti-Gay | |
Year	UCR	ADL	UCR	NCAVP
2000	1,109	1,606	1,299	2135
2001	1,043	1,432	1,393	1943
2002	931	1,559	1,244	1968
2003	927	1,557	1,239	1720
2004	954	1,821	1,197	1792
2005	848	1,757	1,017	1440
2006	967	1,554	1,195	1486

Sources: Anti-Defamation League, 2007; 2006; 2005; 2004; 2003; 2002; 2001; National Coalition of Anti-Violence Programs, 2007; 2006; 2005; 2004; 2003; 2002; 2001

That the UCR data dramatically under-represent the magnitude of hate crime is evident. For both categories of bias motivated violence, the number of incidents recorded in the UCR is far below those reported to the specific agencies. This disparity is especially evident in the comparison between the UCR and the data collected by the National Coalition of Anti-Violence Programs (NCAVP), which represents only select urban centers across the country.

Bell (forthcoming) identifies an array of structural limitations on police recording of hate crime:

> Different levels of organizational procedure exist around hate crimes. In order to be reported, hate crimes must be recognized, counted, and eventually reported. There are vast differences between police departments whether, the degree to which, and in what way officers are trained. Training specifically focused on hate crime factors often leads to increased hate crime reporting. Other institutional factors which increase hate crime reporting include the level of supervision in crime investigations and whether there is departmental policy regarding hate crimes.

Similar conclusions are drawn by Nolan et al. (forthcoming):

> In addition, police officers themselves sometimes may not want to invest extensive time and energy investigating hate crimes because of personal prejudices, lack of training, or organizational policies and practices that reward and promote officers for serious in-progress felony arrests or life-

saving heroics rather than their ability to mediate or prevent inter-group conflict.

Significantly, both Bell and Nolan et al. acknowledge that department level policies alone cannot account for the lack of attention directed toward hate crime. Rather, the decisions of individual officers—as "first responders" and "investigators"—also play a pivotal role in shaping hate crime statistics. Table 5.2 below offers an overview of the decision points with respect to hate crime recording. As first responders and investigators, police officers have tremendous discretion in whether to a) report and incident and b) investigate it further. Unfortunately, there is ample evidence–beginning with the data presented above—to suggest that police are, in fact, hesitant to do either (Bell, 2002, forthcoming; Nolan et al., 1999, forthcoming; Parker, forthcoming).

Table 5.2
The Hate Crime Reporting Process

Decision Maker	*Action*
Victim	Recognize Report
First Responder *(Police)*	Recognize Report
Investigators	Verify Charge
Police Records	Database for crime analysis intelligence prevention source for UCR
Victim and Community Services	Assist Victims/Communities prevention intelligence environment that supports reporting hate crimes

Adapted from Nolan et al. (forthcoming)

In one of the earliest studies exploring why police failed to pursue hate crime complaints, Nolan et al (1999) observed that individual attitudes and beliefs about hate crime and hate crime reporting were as significant as the structural dimensions noted above:

> This refers to the officers' personal beliefs about hate crime and hate crime reporting. These personal beliefs include whether hate crime reporting is effective, whether it is the job of the police to do it, or whether the officers believe hate crime is really a problem that needs to be addressed–to name just a few (Nolan et al., 1999: 21).

This research and subsequent work by Jeannine Bell (2002; forthcoming) reveals that many officers do not see hate crime as a "legitimate" category of crime, and instead see allegations of hate crime as little more than political ploys. Thus, even the efforts of those who are assigned to—or even personally committed to—the investigation of hate crime (e.g., via specialized Bias Crime Units) are commonly thwarted by unsupportive peers.

Additionally, police indirectly play a role in the very first decision point, that is, in whether the victim decides to report the incident. Given the uneasy relationship between police and Native Americans addressed throughout this text, and the immediately forgoing problems associated with policing of hate crime specifically, it is not surprising that, more than any other theme, participants overwhelmingly felt that police failed to take seriously their complaints of victimization. Indeed, many participants in the study complained of the under-enforcement of the law against those threatening American Indians. Not only are police gatekeepers in the process of deciding who is "a criminal," so too do they play the lead role in determining who is "a victim." According to participants, it is not a role they play with neutrality, but with clear biases as to the (il)legitimacy of Native American complainants:

> Well, even the city, they'll say, "oh another complaint, same thing." So they're already biased, not taking each individual report. At least do the basics, writing down what happened, go through the motions at least—at least do that. But their mind's already biased, oh another complaining Indian. So they don't care, won't act on it (Female, Wisconsin).

There appeared to be broad consensus as to the unwillingness of police to respond to American Indian concerns—so much so, that the general sentiment is that it's not worth the effort to even report victimization to police:

> Q. I'm just wondering if you think that people report the problems, if they report to police.
> A. I don't really think so because, I mean, the system's already set up, you know, if you go from point A to point B, they might just throw it away. The police don't listen; they don't file a report or papers or anything. If it goes higher, then it gets lost or whatever or thrown out because the police didn't look into, there's nothing to support the charge. Why bother if you're going to be losing out in the end anyway? There's always the thought that you are going to lose. Like with that highway patrol case. You just throw in your towel and say, "I'd rather pay the lower fine than the higher fine even it it's not right" (Female, Montana).

> When Indian people become a victim, they don't know where to go or who to see to remedy the situation. So at that point, Native people become angry and frustrated, and that particular situation does not get resolved, and the Native people say, "Oh, what the heck!" When Native people do get an opportunity to file a complaint, it's always a negative reply. Native people don't trust the White system, because it's always in their favor, so they figure it's a losing battle right from the start (Male, Minnesota).

In part, this is perceived to be a reflection of points raised earlier. For instance, law enforcement are thought to draw on stereotypes to justify "shortcuts" in investigations:

> You see a lot of that in the park—somebody mistreating someone, and it's always, like, young white people attacking older Native Americans, and that happens in the park. We've had several Navajo people that have died in the park, and I think one time my dad was involved, he kind of got attacked in the park by non-Indians, but we were very fortunate to just drive up then, so they ran. But we told the police and they said there was nothing they could do. There wasn't any "evidence." And so usually when the Navajo die in the park it's written off as "alcohol poisoning" or something. They don't want to ask questions (Female, Arizona).

> A. Yeah, it's not investigated because the police, they'll all just, you know the influence they have over the medical people, etc. so they'll say it was alcohol poisoning or something—of course, it's an Indian it's alcohol and people believe it. So we're seeing a lot of those problems too (Female, Arizona).

Moreover, this appears to hold true across the spectrum of violence. That is, police are thought to be equally non-responsive to minor problems such as automobile accidents, or harassment as they are to much more serious threats to physical safety. The former is apparent in the following narratives:

> When I came home with the bullet holes in my house, I said, "hey, you better send somebody out here, my house is all shot up" well, four hours later, they got somebody out there, another time, I wasn't home, I was gone someplace, somebody was trying to break in, one of the neighbors came up on it and said, "hey, what the hell are you guys doing, just stop right here" and his mom lived right across the street and, she was out there and told his mom, "well, you better call the cops, because these people are trying to break in here" and, so, she went in to call the cops, two and a half hours later, they hadn't come out yet, and everybody was just tired of waiting, so they just let him go, well, he doesn't know if they even came out (Male, Minnesota).

> The heck of it is that a lot of the older students that are doing it—I'll strain myself here and call them rednecks—their grandpa is the mayor or uncle is on county board or cousin is sheriff, their folks might be in town government. So they were really "pillars of the community." It didn't make things any easier. Law enforcement was pretty reluctant to do anything. Their jobs would be more or less to smooth things over for the moment so they didn't address the problem (Male, Wisconsin).

> These people, they don't react to any kind of emergency, take their time and tell you they got more important things to take care of. A guy went off the road, and went into some brush, I don't think he hit anything, he just stopped. But you never know if he's hurt. And I called the police and twenty-nine minutes later here comes the highway patrol—twenty-nine minutes later! And it's three minutes out of town! . . . They don't respond at all; they sit here and they visit and drink coffee, and it's like, what about the highways, you know? And they say "our officers are very efficient and

they respond to this and that." Well they don't respond to us (Male, Minnesota).

Even more disturbing, however, is the contention that they don't take violent victimization seriously either. Again, there was a widespread belief that police were less than thorough in investigating violent deaths and homicides of Native American victims. Two participants who were interviewed together strung together a litany of un- or under-investigated deaths in the Northern Plains, stating that "it's nothing new. Since first contact, dead Indians haven't drawn much attention." Similar sentiments were evident in interviews in the midwest:

> We had two deaths, unfounded deaths here in the community. Two girls have been killed. I called the tribal chairman and I asked what was going on with that. I said the white girl, which a lot of white girls are beaten and killed by men, and they continued a upspeeded investigation to find out who did it. That hasn't happened with the Indians. We still have two unsolved murders. The murderers are walking around on our reservation, if that's what it is (Female, Montana).

> You really see it now, after those two elderly people were killed. The police are all over that, as they should be. It was really a bad thing to happen. But they never really did anything when my nephew was killed a while back. When white people get killed everybody wants to know who, and to catch 'em, especially if they think it was an Indian. But not when an Indian gets *killed*. They didn't go to any great lengths to find who did it, or anything. *Now,* this white couple gets killed and they wanna do something; *now* they say there's a violence problem around here. What they mean is, now the white folks are in danger, we got a problem (Female, Montana).

Moreover, concrete experiences of Native Americans interviewed confirm these perceptions. Many participants reported lack of police intervention, even in the face of imminent danger. One of the most dramatic examples follows:

> I don't know if you ever had a guy standing thirty feet away, holding a loaded shotgun aimed at your head, you ever had that experience, it's not, well, it's something that sticks with you for a while, you know? . . . Well, my wife was there, and I said "you better go get some help." So she went and called the county sheriff, so unless there's been retrocession, you know, the state has jurisdiction on the reservation, criminal jurisdiction, and uh, so she went and called the cops, and it didn't actually take them that long, you know, fifteen, twenty minutes later here comes a county sheriff deputy, comes rolling up, he looks at the situation, he looks at this dude standing there holding a shotgun, and I'm standing in one spot, because I don't want to move, and he's drunk, and the county cop looks at it and says, I don't have any jurisdiction here, and gets in his car and drives away. And he was getting madder, he wasn't cooling off, he was getting more and more worked up as this thing was unfolding and so, as this thing went on and on and on, she finally said, okay. We had reservation officers, tribal game wardens; she said "I'll go see if I can get one of them up here." I couldn't believe it. I batted zero that day, because he walked up, or drove

up, he had his uniform, he had his gun, he had his truck, he had the full thing. *He* looked at it and said, "this is not my jurisdiction." And *he* went on his way. Finally, the guy, this was going on for like an hour and a half or two hours, and I was "oh man!" Finally I think the guy had to take a leak or something . . . "Not my jurisdiction!" I couldn't believe I was gonna die and that's all they could say (Male, Wisconsin).

In this case, and others like it, the failure of law enforcement to intervene in events unfolding before their very eyes could easily have had fatal consequences for the potential victims. In the eyes of Native Americans, the willingness of police to take such a risk signals the relative worth of American Indian lives.

The malign neglect of Native American victimization leaves communities vulnerable, cutting off as it does access to the protections afforded non-Native victims of crime. These negligent practices extend a powerful message and justification for the violent marginalization of Native American victims of crime. They signal to perpetrators, criminal justice personnel and the rest of society that anti-Indian violence will not be punished. While it is bad enough that law enforcement condones victimization by inaction, in some cases they step further over that line, actively facilitating violence by word and deed. This was especially evident throughout the midwestern spear-fishing conflicts of the 1980s and 1990s where police acted in sympathy with the protesters, against Native American spear-fishers. The police response was disturbingly reminiscent of police involvement in lynchings or in the Klan earlier in the century. So apparent were the parallels that many Wisconsin interviewees referred to their state as the Deep North. Indeed, anti-Indian demonstrators could rely on the complicity and support of law enforcement in their harassment of Native spear-fishers and their supporters:

My mother took a jacket with a hood and put it over and started to disguise herself and sort of infiltrated the anti-Indian group. She made her way towards the law enforcement area—they were talking—because it was rather tense. The leadership was talking amongst themselves about what they would do if any violence broke out, for example, and they were all looking towards this talker for guidance, and basically what the question was, if violence breaks out, what should we do? And the gentleman stated frankly, "protect the whites!" And my mother did not know who this guy was until a couple of days later, there was a news story about Lieut. Gov. Scott McCallum and she said "that's him, the guy who said that" (Male, Wisconsin).

And, in fact, it appeared to onlookers that "protect the whites" they did—not the Native spear-fishers. In spite of the hundreds of incidents of death threats, vandalism, guns and wrist rockets fired, rocks thrown and more, over the course of several years in the late 1980s and early 1990s, police made very few arrests of protestors. This generally occurred only in the most blatant of cases, as when police cruisers were rammed, or office themselves somehow affected (Whaley and Bressette, 1994). Clearly, the Natives were not deemed worthy of protection. Police were in sympathy with protestors' assertions of "special rights" and "overfishing" among the Chippewa, such that protestors could readily violate Native peoples' basic human rights to be free from threat and personal injury.

In contrast—and in line with my previous argument about *over-policing* Native Americans—police were thought to be eager to intervene *on behalf of* protestors. One Native activist describes two such cases, where police acceded to protestors' requests to arrest Native Americans and their supporters:

> My husband was arrested along with another man for holding up the Plains Indian flag at a boat landing. Well, we forgot to tell you the whole point of that story, which is: the protestors had ordered the police to arrest them! And as it turned out, they had them in a back of a squad car, and there was frantic radio communication back and forth to try to find something to charge them with! AND a friend and treaty rights supporter was also arrested at a joint PARR/STA rally at Torpy Park in Minocqua for holding up a sign reading People Already Racist (and) Radical (PARR) and we were ALL there and the PARR speakers actually *ordered* the law enforcement to arrest her even though all she was doing was silently standing there holding up a sign! And the police, at PARR's direction, did arrest her! The main points are that in those times the police were actually being manipulated by the anti-Indian groups! And very openly, as the man who called for her arrest did so by microphone from a stage (Female, Wisconsin).

Policing Violence against Aboriginal Women

The difficulty of police inattention to indigenous victims of crime is amplified when those victims are women. Indeed, Chris Cunneen (2001: 161) claims that "the question of over-policing is misconceived if it fails to consider the fact that the levels of violence perpetrated against Aboriginal women do not receive attention from police authorities. In the arena of protecting women the issue has been identified as one of *under-policing*." Research in Canada, Australia, and the United States have consistently established the enhanced vulnerability of indigenous women on the basis of intersecting systems of oppression. In Australia, the extent and severity of the problem is visible from any number of government sponsored commissions and inquiries, such as the Royal Commission into Aboriginal Deaths, the National Inquiry into Racist Violence, and the Western Australian Chief Justice's Taskforce on Gender Bias, Human Rights and Equal Opportunity Commission Report. Provincial commissions across Canada have likewise established both the widespread racialized and gendered violence against Aboriginal women, and the lack of adequate police response to the same (most notably in Manitoba). In contrast, American evidence is largely drawn from independent research projects, that nonetheless come to the same daunting conclusions (Bubar and Thurman, 2004; Smith 2005; Hurtado, 1997; Faery, 1999).

The seriousness of this problem is evident in the very high incidence of violence against indigenous women. Rates of violent victimization are higher for Native American women than for all other groups across the country, and the disparity seems to be greatest in rural areas in and around reservations (Perry, 2004), the very areas where the police presence is lowest, and where police attention to Indian victimization is also lowest.

Victimization of women and girls, in particular, had long been part of the arsenal of violence used to contain Native Americans (Smith, 2005), and might in fact be characterized as intrinsic to the processes of genocide and decimation that accompany colonization. A growing body of literature attests to the destructive impact that such violence has on women and on the larger community (Cunneen, 2001; Hurtado, 1997; Faery, 1999). A people cannot last long when its women come under attack. The most methodical of the "Indian-haters," Andrew Jackson recognized this as a "wise" military strategy. He encouraged armies to be sure that they killed all women and children that could be found after a battle, since it was akin to hunting "a wolf in the hammocks without knowing first where her den and whelps were" (cited in Stannard, 1992: 122). In other words, the large scale murders of women would minimize the reproductive capacities of any given village or tribe. This was precisely what was wanted: to shrink the Indian population to nothing over the course of time. Moreover, sexual assaults on women by colonizers can be seen as an attempt to minimize the power of men and of the community as a whole. Moreover, such efforts helped in the erosion of traditional lifeways grounded in respect for women (and nature), replacing them with European models of patriarchy and the devaluing of women (and nature) (Bubar and Thurman, 2004; Smith 2005).

As the processes of colonization became even more brutal and more self-consciously genocidal in intent, women would continue to suffer loss of life and dignity at the hands of military troops bent on the destruction of entire communities. This was alluded to earlier in the reference to Andrew Jackson. According to contemporary literature on human rights violations against women, this is arguably one of the most heinous ways by which to wage "war" against the enemy (Bunch, 1995; Nenadic, 1996; Rittner, 2002). War time rapes of civilian women are indisputably acts of domination. But they are as much about racial and ethnic domination as about gender domination in this context. Moreover, it is not the act of undisciplined individuals; rather it is a systematic means of humiliating and subjugating a population. It is part of, rather than a consequence of war, to the extent that rape occurs during military assaults in much the same way that assaults on villages or farms might be—as standard means of weakening the community.

Historically, then, agents of the state have been complicit in the subjugation of indigenous women. The pattern continues today by different means. As the previous chapter indicated, police are not themselves above victimizing vulnerable women. However, they also facilitate violence by creating an enabling environment through negligence. Unfortunately, this is not something I thought to fully examine in my interviews. Nonetheless, this is one area of police-Native American relations that has garnered some academic interest. A recent Canadian study, for example, found indigenous women to be very dissatisfied with police responses to their complaints of violence at the hands of their partners (McGillivray and Comaskey, 2004). Two respondents provided especially powerful testimony to the tendency of police to deny the harm to the victims. Both had called the police so frequently—with little impact on their situations—that the police response was to become angry at them.

> One time when I called the police, the staff sergeant was upset with me. He says, "I'm getting pretty upset with you, you're always phoning, calling here, you're getting to be a bloody nuisance . . . I should charge you for harassing, phoning here all the time."

> They always seemed like they were getting disgusted with you, because it is repeated over and over again, being abused and then charge him, and then it would happen again, being abused and then I would charge him. Pretty soon it seemed like even the police got tired of it and didn't take it seriously anymore (in McGillivray and Comaskey, 2004: 96).

Rather than take seriously their ongoing vulnerability, the officers in question berated *the victims* for harassing *the police*. In so doing, they dismissed both the credibility and the voices of the victims.

Another illustrative example comes from the Canadian trial of Frank Kim, who was ultimately convicted on twenty-seven counts of an array of violent crimes committed against nine young girls, six of whom were Aboriginal. The number of offenses he was able to perpetrate against these teenagers was undoubtedly extended by inappropriate actions which amounted to under-policing and hence under-protecting the victims. Police action/inaction that demonstrated a lack of careful investigation included

- Kim was pulled over with a group of teenage girls in his car and the police failed to question him about this suspicious situation. Instead, they focused on a seatbelt infraction.
- The police failed to treat Kim as suspicious when one of his victims tried to escape from Kim by taking his car. Despite the fact that there was an obvious desire of this Aboriginal young woman to get away from Kim, the police responded to her as a criminal.
- A young woman who was raped by Kim reported the rape to police and yet the police failed to question Kim even though the young woman told police his identity and address.
- The police released a twelve-year-old Aboriginal girl, a victim of Frank Kim, onto the street in the early hours of the morning after interrogating her about Kim's abuse.

This reflects the tendency noted above to identify "deserving" and "undeserving" victims. Here, indigenous women are found to be at fault for their own victimization. The message to Native women "is that they are expendable and there is no real help or assistance within the system" (Bubar and Thurman, 2004: 78).

Note, earlier, that I mentioned the ways in which Native Americans are held by police officers to be inherently "troublesome." This may extend, too, to their ineffectual response to intra-racial violence against indigenous women. Where Native American men, in particular, are presumed criminal, it is no surprise that they behave violently toward women. This is "only natural," it is normative within the stigmatized culture. Adelman et al. (2003: 115-116) surveyed the relevant literature on policing violence against minority women generally and found consistently that there exists "a patriarchal male fraternity and identification between law enforcement officials and minority men whose communities they serve, predisposing police officers to overlook the harm, or question the credibility of abused women's complaints."

Police apathy with respect to victimization of Native Americans— women and men alike—is yet another element of the disparate and racialized treatment they mete out to this community. What has been implicit in chapters 5 and 6, is that the cumulative practices of over- and under-policing Native American communities comes with a high price not just for the affected individuals and their communities, but also for police and for the justice system generally. I take up this question of the impacts of disparate policing in the following chapter.

Chapter 6
Impacts of Disparate Policing

Inevitably, the experiences of Native Americans like those whose voices are shared here shape their perceptions of the brand of justice they can expect. Cumulatively, over- and under-policing reinforce the antipathy if not outright hostility toward police. They compound the historically strained relationship between Native Americans and the western criminal justice system. Yet the impacts of disparate policing also have broader community and political effects, including disempowerment, segregation, and enhanced risk of victimization.

Native Americans are not alone in facing the burden imposed by racially discriminatory police practices. A 2002 Leadership Conference on Civil Rights report entitled *Justice on Trial: Racial Disparities in the American Criminal Justice System* documented the widespread disparities faced by African Americans and Hispanic Americans in particular. Importantly, the report also highlighted the cumulative consequences of these inequities. Four key areas were identified:

1. disempowerment of minority communities;
2. exacerbation of minority hostility and distrust toward the justice system;
3. impact on minority communities in terms of economics and public health; and
4. loss of national ideals.

A later report from Amnesty International stressed similar debilitating effects, arguing that the "human impact" of disparate police behaviors culminates in diminished trust in police, and disempowered and disenfranchised communities (Amnesty International, 2004). Interestingly, a 2003 Ontario Human Rights Commission inquiry on the "human cost" of racial profiling specifically saw fit to devote a component of the inquiry and report to the specific experiences of Aboriginal people in Ontario. This was justified with reference to the unique historical and political situation of Canada's First Nations, and to the recognition that they were not "just another ethnic minority group," but rather constituted nations unto themselves. Regardless of the race of the affected community however, the inquiry came to similar conclusions as those in the American reports. Racial profiling has devastating effects on the emotional, psychological, financial, physical, even cultural well-being of not just the affected individuals but their communities as well (Ontario Human Rights Commission, 2003).

Together, the reports make it clear that the historical and contemporary experiences of racialized groups with respect to the American (in)justice system has led to a diminution of the strength of these communities. With respect to Native American communities, specifically, such experiences extend the historical practices of colonialism noted in chapter 3. As such, police mistreatment limits the ability and willingness of communities to participate in the broader patterns of social and political life. It has left them with unstable families, limited economic resources, and similarly limited social and cultural capital. Moreover, it has attenuated the long-standing distrust of the criminal justice system—and the dominant culture generally—to the extent that members of black, Latino, Asian, and certainly Native American communities are unwilling to cooperate with a system that reinforces their oppression. Indeed, the interviews that I conducted revealed evidence of similar impacts and reactions among Native American communities. In what follows, I highlight the key themes noted by participants.

Over-representation

The Leadership Conference document cited above draws the inevitable conclusion, with respect to African Americans and Latinos, that there is a "cyclical quality" to the disparate policing of these communities. Police distrust of blacks and Latinos causes a

> disproportionate share of law enforcement attention to be directed at minorities, which in turn leads to more arrests of blacks and Hispanics. Disproportionate arrests fuel prosecutorial and judicial decisions that disproportionately affect minorities and result in disproportionate incarceration rates for minorities (Leadership Conference on Civil Rights, 2002: online).

The same holds true for Native Americans. The sort of over-zealous surveillance and excessive contact discussed in chapter 4 results in a heightened risk of arrest and sanction. I noted early in this work that police are the front line of the criminal justice system, that they initiate the process of criminalization of racial minorities. Their actions and decisions provide the disproportionate "sample" from which the later legal category of criminal is drawn. Indeed, across the United States, and especially in those states where Native Americans make up a sizable proportion of the population, they are over-represented in arrest and correctional statistics. Nationally, American Indians make up approximately 1% of the population; yet they consistently account for about 15% of offenders entering federal prisons. Between 1977 and 2002, they represented 13.3% of executed prisoners, and in 2002, 45% of those on death row. In all, over 4% of the Native American population is under correctional supervision on any given day—contrasted with 2% of the white population (Bureau of Justice

Statistics, 2004). In all but one of the states included in my project, American Indians are dramatically over-represented in state prisons and jails (see table 6.1). In New Mexico, their representation is more or less proportionate, although some counties and towns with high Native populations do have disproportionate numbers of Native Americans in their jails (e.g., San Juan County, Farmington).

Table 6.1
Native American Incarceration Rate by State

STATE	POPULATION (%)	INCARCERATION IN STATE PRISONS AND JAILS (%)
Arizona	5.0	6.3
Colorado	1.0	3.4
Minnesota	1.1	7.6
Montana	6.2	20.5
Utah	1.3	5.2
Wisconsin	0.9	3.9

Source: *Prison Policy Initiative*
(www.prisonpolicy.org/graphs/statepopulations.html)

These are trends of which community members are well aware.

Um, well, if you look at the *Lake Powell Chronicle* you know, under the police report, you'll see mostly Native Americans, for minor traffic violations, you see them in Tuba City and Kayenta, and Page, all over, but you hardly see Anglo peoples' names in there, so you know they're looking for Native Americans on the street; I see that (Male, Arizona).

I see it around me. I would bet dollars that if you took an inventory of who the police stop, who they take into custody—Red Cliff tribe is probably less than 10% of the population at any given point—it is 75 or 90% maybe some days 100% of the population police deal with. It's hard to put your finger on something that says this is racial profiling or discrimination, or this is the outcome of some sort of bias or prejudice. I think it is, but it's very difficult to *prove cause*. But in the end, it means more of us are in jail (Male, Wisconsin).

The primary impact of over-policing Native American communities, then, is disproportionate rates of arrest and formal sanctions. As noted above, Native Americans represent a substantial number of federal, state, and local inmates, often criminalized for relatively minor offenses.

In short, disparate policing is among those mechanisms by which Native American individuals and communities become criminalized. The heightened surveillance and excessive zeal with which law enforcement appears to enforce the law in Indian Country means that they are disproportionately caught in the web of social control. In the now classic *Policing the Crisis*, Hall et al. (1978: 38) capture the essence of this process:

"The paradox is that the selectivity of police reaction to select crimes"—and one might add criminals—"almost certainly serves to *increase* their numbers." More than a decade later, a Canadian justice inquiry drew a similar conclusion: "We believe that Aboriginal people are arrested and held in custody when a white person in the same circumstances either might not be arrested at all or might not be held" (Hamilton and Sinclair, 1991: 595). The narratives of my participants suggest that little has changed since.

So widespread are the practices of racial profiling and elevated surveillance in and around reservations that virtually all participants noted them. Consequently, a corollary effect of excessive police attention to Native American offending is the exacerbation of hostility and distrust of law enforcement generally.

Fostering Hostility and Distrust

There's a lot of incidents that never get reported—who ya' gonna file a complaint with: The County? The State? The Feds? Nobody trusts them, they're a big part of the problem (Male, Montana).

Given the evidence presented throughout this text, it should come as no surprise that many Native Americans hold negative perceptions of law enforcement. Inevitably, the direct and indirect experiences of Native Americans like those I interviewed shape their perceptions of the fairness and value of the criminal justice system and law enforcement. Interestingly, this resonates with a recent study of African American experiences with aggressive policing. Rod Brunson's (2007) interviews with black urban males offers up evidence of the cumulative impact of such (mis)treatment. His fundamental conclusion was that the "combination of frequent involuntary contact, coupled with what study participants considered poor treatment during such encounters, contributed to an accumulated body of unfavorable experiences that collectively shaped young men's views of police" (Brunson, 2007: 95).

In fact, many Native Americans are very explicit about their perceptions of the blatancy of police discrimination, and their reaction to this. A young male from New Mexico stated openly that "police make life pure hell for Native Americans in the community, 'cause there's a lot of problems with discrimination on the part of the police officers." Participants were very much aware of—and angered by—what they saw as differential treatment of Whites and Natives:

It's like I don't know, they slap you in the back of the car real quick. They think you're going to run off on them or something. Where like a white kid man, they just take you in the school and speak to you in the office. They'll slap me in the car, and they just try to talk to the teachers (Male, Montana).

It's just amazing, talking now, you know, one of my nieces was thrown in jail, and she said that she witnessed the Indian kids getting thrown in but the white kids getting to go, it's different treatment, I could get pulled over going five miles over the speed limit, the sign's right there, I'll get a ticket, you hear a white person here say that they let them go every time, we live on third street and I see the police officers here making Indians get out and demanding, "you call me Sir" it's really an abuse. Yeah, the prejudice in Harden is, I mean, it's blatant, you don't escape it, everyday it's totally different treatment. (Female, Montana).

One man from Montana seemed to want to give police the benefit of the doubt, but ultimately revealed that he shared the same perception of unequal treatment at the hands of law enforcement:

So, as far as the, the police, I think that they try to apply the laws as equally as possible, but there again, you still have a line, who does this apply to, it doesn't apply to this person, that kind of thing goes on all the time because the people here in town have been behaving like that for years and years, so why should they change now? (Male, Arizona)

As others attested, there was indeed a sense that the law was not applied equally. Rather, "who this applies to" was generally thought to be Native Americans, and rarely Whites. These observed patterns serve to reinforce the antipathy toward police and to deepen the cycle of hostility that characterizes police-community relations. One youth expressed the sentiment most concisely: "We hate them because they hate us." Ongoing disparities in policing provoke an intense dislike of police officers:

Cops are jerks around here. Nobody likes 'em.
Yeah, I hate the cops around here 'cause they're always watching us.
Yeah, it ain't right the way they treat us. No wonder everybody hates them. They just aren't fair (Males and Females, Minnesota).

The underlying sense of inequity that evokes this hostility also undermines the community's faith in police, and in the justice system more broadly. The legacy of "massive injustices inevitably breeds consequences. When any minority group experiences injustice at the hands of dominant society, anger, frustration, and agony are bred. More than a century of . . . injustice on a massive scale has induced a chronic sense of oppression among Indians" (Boldt, 1993: 60). Understandably, police are often perceived as key agents in historical and contemporary patterns of oppression; they are representative of a culture that has so often betrayed them. Consequently, they are often the focus of precisely the anger and frustration to which Boldt refers. As the opening quote of this section implies, rather than foster trust and respect, they garner the opposite in light of their simultaneous tendencies to both under- and over-police Native American communities. The recollections of many participants in this study confirm this precarious relationship:

I think they don't trust us, that's why we get stopped, especially kids. They think they're doing something. So it makes sense we don't trust them too. It's like us against them. I'm not gonna call police if I think they won't believe me (Female, Montana).

They don't deserve our support. I won't help police 'cause I don't think
they wanna help us. You can't depend on them to come if you call, or to
do anything even if they do (Male, Wisconsin).

None of my friends will trust 'em. Nobody wants to be a cop 'cause they
know then we won't talk to them. Nobody want to be seen as one of them,
as somebody who you can't talk to. Don't blame 'em, because they just
don't care about us (Male, Minnesota).

Research among African American communities, in particular, has
established the damaging effects of community distrust of police on the
justice system. The LCCR (2002) report noted earlier speaks to this, placing
particular emphasis on the loss of the moral authority of the law. The report
also cites the unwillingness of affected communities to participate in the
justice system as victims, witnesses or jurors. Similar conclusions were
drawn by the OHRC (2003) report on Canadian minority group perceptions
of Canadian justice:

The social cost of creating mistrust of institutions includes a lack of
respect shown to people associated with them, greater acting out against
those institutions or the law, and an unwillingness to work with those
institutions, for example, by reporting crime, acting as witnesses, etc.
(OHRC, 2003: 29).

In light of my arguments in chapter 3 above, it is important that perceptions
of police antipathy, harassment, and violence be seen through the prism of
American Indians' social and individual histories. For them, any one
incident of police mistreatment adds to the ledger of racism (Varma-Joshi,
Baker, and Tanaka, 2004: 191). As Varma-Joshi et al. (2004: 191) describe
it, Indigenous people experience racist harassment and violence within the
context of the history of colonization, and segregation, and within the
context of their own lifelong experiences of similar incidents. The combined
personal and cultural biographies cultivate a sense of intergenerational grief
and trauma which, according to Bubar and Thurman (2004: 74), "are the
psychological fallout from federal policies that demeaned Native culture and
used violence to force assimilation." It is, moreover, the correspondence of
the individual and the collective experience that both problematizes the
treatment, while at the same time rendering it normative. As an indelible
part of their history, Native Americans come to expect harassment and
violence whenever they come in contact with white people generally, and
police officers specifically.

The historical embeddedness of the uneasy relationship between police
and Native Americans means that current exchanges are inevitably seen as
"more of the same." Recall the words of the Arizona man cited above, who
says that "people here in town have been behaving like that for years and
years, so why should they change now?" Contemporary police practices are
seen as an extension of centuries of harassment, violence and containment
that have long limited the capacities of Native American individuals and

communities. In short, the distrust and hostility documented here has the related effect of marginalizing and disempowering Native Americans.

Marginalization and Disempowerment

Elsewhere, I have referred to the ways in which hate crime is constitutive of and by an inter-connected web of oppression (Perry, forthcoming). Following Iris Marion Young's (1990) framework, I argue that hate crime—what Young might consider systemic violence—is one among five "faces of oppression" that also includes cultural imperialism, exploitation, marginalization and disempowerment. I characterize the relationships among and between these factors as follows:

> The first three of these mechanisms reflect the structural and institutional relationships which restrict opportunities for minority groups to express their capacities and to participate in the social world around them. It is the processes and imagery associated with cultural imperialism which support these practices ideologically. Together, structural exclusions and cultural imaging leave minority members vulnerable to systemic violence, and especially hate crime (Perry, forthcoming).

The opposite can also be said, that is, systemic violence perpetuates the barriers to participation and engagement. And the same can be said for the sort of disparate policing noted in this text. It, too, is embedded in the historical and contemporary systems of disadvantage confronted by Native Americans. Indeed, it might well be seen as a form of systemic violence in and of itself.

In particular, Native American experiences with police officers have dramatic consequences for the exacerbation of centuries long patterns of marginalization and disempowerment. Consequently, their sense of being a valued part of American society is dramatically curtailed. Rather than seeing themselves as embedded in the polity and culture of the United States, many Native Americans come to see themselves and their communities as outside the boundaries of citizenship and its attendant rights. This emerges first and foremost in the context of the police-citizen interaction itself.

Miller (1996: 99) observes that, for young men of color, contact with police "comes with deep, historical racially anchored roots and turns into an internal psychological struggle over whether to meekly assume or aggressively reject the identity the ritual demands." All too often, Native Americans try to avoid the "ritual" exchange entirely. Thus, a very common reaction is to cease to engage with law enforcement, effectively forfeiting one's right to protection:

> When Indian people become a victim, they don't know where to go or who to see to remedy the situation. So at that point, Native people become angry and frustrated, and that particular situation does not get resolved, and the Native people say, "Oh, what the heck!" When Native people do get an opportunity to file a complaint, it's always a negative reply. Native

people don't trust the White system, because it's always in their favor, so they figure it's a losing battle right from the start (Male, Minnesota).

Q. I'm just wondering if you think that people report the problems, if they report to police.
A. I don't really think so because, I mean, the system's already set up, you know, if you go from point A to point B, they might just throw it away. The police don't listen; they don't file a report or papers or anything. If it goes higher, then it gets lost or whatever or thrown out because the police didn't look into, there's nothing to support the charge. Why bother if you're going to be losing out in the end anyway? There's always the thought that you are going to lose. Like with that highway patrol case. You just throw in your towel and say, "I'd rather pay the lower fine than the higher fine even it it's not right" (Female, Montana).

In other words, the perception of recurrent negligence, harassment, and victimization leaves its subjects feeling disempowered. They feel themselves to be without a voice, without an avenue to justice. They feel marginal at best, violently constrained at worst. At the very least, it limits their desire to interact with white people, and certainly with police.

Exacerbating the unwillingness to report to law enforcement is the fear of police officers themselves. The opening quote in this section draws attention to this concern. On the one hand, Native American victims rightly fear police apathy. More significantly, however, they also have reason to fear violence on the part of police. The evidence of police brutality presented in chapter 4 sets the context for this. Whether victims, suspects, witnesses or innocent bystanders, Native Americans often hesitate to draw attention to themselves for fear of police harassment, whether verbal, physical, or even sexual. Youth, in particular, shared their fear of police violence. For example,

Especially if there's more than a couple of us, police will watch us, follow us. They've thrown me in the car and roughed me up. I don't wanna be near them (Male, Montana).

For some, such encounters angered them into defensive responses; for most, however, it seemed to reinforce the message that Native Americans should remain silent even in the face of victimization:

I don't want that to happen to me, for them to hit me, or kick me. I won't go to the police. I won't talk to 'em, 'cause ya' just don't know where that's gonna go. I guess only if I end up in the hospital will I tell police about being a victim (Female, Wisconsin).

Aside from minimizing the likelihood of reporting their victimization, racialized patterns of policing have another more serious consequence to the extent that over-policing, in particular, culminates in political disempowerment. On the one hand, the very experiences across the continuum from police harassment and violence to police neglect leave their victims feeling like "an unequal or less worthy member of society" to the extent that these processes are perceived as "humiliating, dehumanizing and painful" (OHRC, 2003: 30). Those affected—directly or indirectly—by these events feel that their rights are somehow less secure than their white counterparts. Disparate police action, then, reinforces their sense of social and political marginality, according to which victims are made to feel like second class citizens. This appears to be especially disturbing for Native Americans:

> My people belong on this land; this was our land before the White folks came. But now, now, I don't feel like I belong here, and especially off the rez. When they stop you at the bridge, they are saying that we are not a part of the community. We don't have the same right to go where we want (Male, Montana).

A sense of belonging is crucial to social inclusion. Yet Native Americans are frequently reminded by bearers of state power that they do not warrant the same recognition or protections as their white counterparts. The sense of alienation emanating from this exclusion can be debilitating to the extent that it has the potential to promote withdrawal from engagement with the broader society, in that "persons who do not feel valued in society cannot contribute or participate to their full potential" (OHRC, 2003: 34). This foreshadows consideration of the segregating effect of disparate policing which follows. Both effects suggest that Native Americans are discouraged from reaching across cultural—or geopolitical—boundaries to participate in political or social activities.

Additionally, I noted above the cyclical nature of police (mis)treatment of Native Americans, in that heightened surveillance is typically accompanied by heightened rates of felony convictions. Consequently, a sizable portion of the Native American community is subject to disenfranchisement. Forty-six states deny the vote to all convicted adults while they are in prison. Twenty-nine disenfranchise those on probation (all of the states included in this study, except Colorado and Montana); and thirty-two states disenfranchise felons on parole (all of the states included in this study, except Montana). Most dramatically, in fourteen states (including Arizona and New Mexico) convicted felons are barred from voting for life.

Consider again the fact that one in twenty-four Native Americans is under correctional control on any given day, either on probation, parole, or in prison. That is a substantial portion of the community that is without political voice. This poses a direct threat to the democratic inclusion of Native American communities. Uggen and Manza (2002: 795), for example, offer a systematic examination of the electoral impact of felony disenfranchisement, showing that

> because the contracted electorate now produces different political outcomes than a fully enfranchised one, mass incarceration and felon disenfranchisement have clearly impeded, and perhaps reversed, the historical extension of voting rights.

Felony disenfranchisement is an extension of historical patterns of restriction on the political participation of racialized minority groups. The communities most in need of a political voice—those that are marginalized and often disadvantaged in myriad ways—are precisely those whose ability to affect change through electoral choices is most dramatically limited. In sum, felony disenfranchisement of Native American offenders reinforces a peculiar form of American apartheid.

Segregation

Elsewhere I have written about the segregating impacts of racially motivated violence directed toward Native Americans (Perry, forthcoming). Generally, racially motivated violence limits their movements and their perceived options, resulting in withdrawal. It creates "more borders," said one participant, in that people become fearful of moving out of the relative safety of the reservation. They "stay here for all their lives, because they're afraid to go 'out there' because of what's going on, for all of these reasons." Very similar sentiments were expressed by others. For example,

> People don't like to go over to Cut Bank, because they don't get treated right, in the stores, in the restaurants, on the streets (Female, Montana)?

For too many American Indians, the perception, if not the reality of "what's out there" has its intended effect of keeping people in their place. It reinforces the boundaries—social and geographical—across which Native Americans are not meant to cross. It contributes to ongoing withdrawal and isolation; in short, it furthers historical patterns of segregation. Through violence, the threat of violence, or even through the malevolent gaze, Native Americans are daily reminded—all too often by the police—that there are places in which they are not welcome.

The process is exacerbated by the (in)actions of police. I wrote at length in chapter 4 about the extensiveness of racial profiling on and near Native American reservations. While not unique to Native Americans, it does have the unique geographical dimension associated with policing reservation boundaries, which become reified by bordering police departments. They take on an inviolable essence that is not to be transgressed. These geopolitical borders take on the nature of an "iron curtain" shielding "us" from "them."

That said, as important as they are for separating "us" from "them," boundaries are nonetheless not truly fixed. In both symbolic and material terms, they are permeable and subject to ongoing tendencies to transgression (Webster, 2003). Native Americans leave the reservation for job opportunities; black Americans move into predominantly white neighborhoods to gain access to better schools and other infrastructural supports; immigrants come to the United States to pursue the "American Dream;" people of color generally demand the right to inclusion and participation in the machineries of economics and politics. As such, they represent threats; they have violated the carefully crafted barriers intended to keep them in their respective boxes. It is in these contexts—at the "symbolic boundaries"—that defensive actions are likely to occur (Webster, 2003: 99). Profiling and disparate police stops thus become territorial defenses of cultural "space."

For reservation Indians, the most important "boundary" separating "us" from "them" is the very real physical boundary that marks the line between Indian land and white land. This is quite literally policed by law enforcement in a way that makes it more than an imaginary geopolitical line, but that gives it the feeling of a wired cage from which Native Americans might escape. Police represent the frontline troops in the effort to maintain the place of racial minorities, in part through practices associated with racial profiling. Few contemporary practices can so effectively serve to put Indians "in their place"—and keep them there. It demonstrates for its subjects—as if they didn't know already—the spatial and cultural boundaries beyond which they must not travel. Racial profiling of Native Americans in and around reservations reinforces the historically conditioned patterns of segregation. This was disturbingly evident in the words of this participant, quoted previously (chapter 4):

> I've seen them just sit there by that bridge—that's the border—and they'll sit here all day and just keep stopping us when we have tribal plates. It's like, as soon as we leave the res, we're stopped for any or no reason. It makes you not wanna leave, you know (Male, Montana)?

This comes as no surprise, since "protecting spatial sovereignty is the primary function of the state," and the police play a dominant role in this strategy (Bass, 2001: 43). Profiling reinforces the spatial partitioning by which Native Americans are "encouraged" to remain within the boundaries of the reservation. And it often has its intended effect, as some participants admitted to changing their behavior in response to this persistent profiling. A woman from Montana exclaimed "And then, on top of it, we'll get harassed by police. As soon as we leave the rez, they're waiting for us. So why would we want to go there?" Consequently, some Native Americans claimed to rarely leave the reservation; others, in areas like Minnesota and Wisconsin, avoided driving near particular reservations or border towns, where they knew police were especially problematic:

> I don't know, yeah, that's, that's the thing like I know in White Earth, you never have your res plates, or don't drive in Bemidji if you have your res plates, like I don't do that very much. They'll pull you over in a heartbeat, you know, if they see you have res plates, you know, for anything small, so yeah, people tend to not have those plates, I don't, just because of that factor. I don't want that chance being pulled over for a stupid minor detail, and the only thing that would be reason, would be my Indian plates, you know? (Female, Minnesota).

Here, it is police action that constrains and threatens Native Americans. Disparate treatment of drivers serves as a constant reminder of where Native

Americans belong. Being "out of place" leaves them vulnerable to police activity. Interestingly, however, police inactivity leaves them vulnerable to different kind of threat, that is, violence.

Enabling Violence

While the disparate policing of Native American communities has a direct impact on arrest and incarceration, as noted above, it also has dramatic implications for the risk of victimization of Native Americans as individuals and as communities. The patterns of policing described herein place Native Americans at an elevated risk of physical danger. This is exacerbated by the perception, also noted above, that Native Americans do not have faith in the willingness or ability of police to intervene, and so are reluctant even to report victimization, even their own. This lesson was apparent to the participant who related the following story:

> Part of it was uh, you know, just the lack of manpower, I remember one really sad and tragic situation, one of these communities, someone got drunk one day, and they had a car and they were just racing and tearing all over the place, just tearing up the town with this car, speeding around, squealing tires, gravel flying, and all this stuff, people tried to call the cops and of course, nobody came, and later that afternoon, you know, a head on car crash with four people killed (Male, Minnesota).

Here is a case of police inaction that had tragic consequences. Yet it is illustrative of the danger posed when police choose not to respond to calls for service.

Another area in which Native American communities are left to fend for themselves is in the context of racially motivated violence. Especially where police fail to intervene, they bestow permission to hate, implying as they do that Native Americans are not worthy of protection (Perry, 2001). As I have argued elsewhere (Perry, 2001), discriminatory practices by the state and by state actors sends a powerful message about the worth—or lack thereof—of its targets. Political discourse and action reaffirms and legitimates the negative evaluations of difference which give rise to hate crime. Thus, I accept van Dijk's (1995: 2) thesis that discourse is central to the "enactment, expression, legitimation and acquisition" of bigotry of all types, including racially motivated violence. Law enforcement agents enact the power of the state and law—and its identity-making capacities—through their actions on Others. State personnel construct identity through ongoing practices which institutionalize specific and normative forms of race. In particular, we have seen that police themselves engage in "derivative deviance," or violence perpetrated on the marked Others who are "presumed unable to avail themselves of civil protection" (Harry, cited in Berrill and Herek, 1992: 290). In other words, the state itself acts as a victimizer, thereby validating the persecution of racialized communities.

Added to this, the common perception that police are not interested in intervening in cases of anti-Indian activity leaves Native Americans feeling vulnerable to ongoing racial harassment and violence. Elsewhere, I have documented and assessed the widespread frequency of racially motivated violence against Native Americans (Perry, 2006; forthcoming). And, in chapter 5, I discussed the perception that police fail to take this victimization seriously, appearing in fact to deny either the reality or the impact of this violence. In sum, police have

> with remarkable consistency denied the racist nature of attacks, played down the seriousness of attacks, often treated victims with hostility and lack of sympathy, allowed alleged attackers to go free, and until recently, refused to make use of their powers to prosecute alleged offenders except in very serious assault cases (Gordon, 2000: 369).

In failing to respond, police are allowing anti-Indian violence to flourish unabated. There is no deterrent when police apathy is seen to be the norm. The following two examples are informative here:

> There was this one guy who followed me and my family around town and in the stores. I finally chased him through a red light because he was trying to push us, shoot us out into other traffic. Finally we stopped at a light and I got out and said "what the hell do you think you're doing?" He had an arrow in his hand and he slammed it down on the hood and broke it and started waving it at me. I chased him around the corner and there was a police officer who just laughed at us, so that was a lot of help. I told him what was going on and he just said "Sounds like you just need to work it out between you." Not an offer of help; he just didn't care. Just another Indian bitching about nothing (Male, Wisconsin).

> Remember when Sarah Bacas got beat up, the police refused to help? They wouldn't help her? They just stared at her like she wasn't there, and she was bleeding and crying! And one time we had a cop tell us at one boat landing, when they were gonna cross over the police line—all that kept them from us was that yellow police tape. And this cop told us "I was ready. If they had crossed over the line, I had my hand on my stick. But I wasn't gonna protect you. I was gonna beat a path for myself to get out of there!" That's the kind of support we got. Somebody documented that a cop or sheriff or something said "If I didn't have this uniform on, I'd be there with them." There were plenty of cases where people were clearly assaulted and the police didn't step in; no charges were ever laid (Female, Wisconsin).

These are blatant examples of the impact of police failure to act. In both cases, perpetrators were able to harass, threaten, or physically assault their victims simply because they could. There was no authoritative intervention that would send the message that their behaviors were in any way unacceptable. On the contrary, they were at least tacitly condoned, thereby granting licence to engage in violence against Native Americans. Such behavior normalizes their mistreatment. Rather than putting an end to the cycle of threat and intimidation, police inaction perpetuates the process:

If the threat of violence and occasional use of actual violence is used to intimidate, exclude, or terrorize, the balance of power between victim and perpetrator remains. Such action, therefore, may be perceived by the victim as a failure of police protection and by the perpetrator as sanctioning his or her actions (Bowling, 1998).

Police inaction—and frequently complicity—reaffirms violence as a means of subjugating Native Americans. It bestows a permission to hate—and to hit.

This chapter has made the argument that there are real consequences—for communities and for police—when law is enforced in visibly disparate ways. It is a major impediment to the relationship between police and Native American communities, and it leaves Native Americans vulnerable to harm and to disempowerment. The question now is what is to be done. Indeed, recent years have seen varied efforts to bridge the gap between racialized minority groups and law enforcement, with uneven results at best. I turn finally in the concluding chapter to a consideration of recent reforms in this context.

Chapter 7
Policing Differently?

Cross-cultural Training for Police Officers

Since at least the 1960s, some form of cultural "awareness" or "sensitivity" training for law enforcement has been seen as a panacea to the hostile relationships between police and racialized communities. Early in the book I referred to findings of decades of commissions and inquiries. Among the recommendations—at least since the Kerner report—have been calls for enhanced understanding and respect for diversity, hence the emphasis on related training. The fact that the most recent commission reports have made the same demands underscores the limited progress that has been made, and also points to the relative ineffectiveness of cultural awareness training.

Interestingly, cultural awareness training programs have been supported by both liberal and conservative reformers, albeit for reasons that are diametrically opposed. For the former, cultural awareness training is seen as a potential inoculant against problems of discrimination, harassment and violence perpetrated by police against racialized and other minority groups. Effective diversity training, they argue, would sensitize police to the impacts of their actions, thereby affecting subsequent changes in their behavior. In contrast, conservative supporters contend that the behavioral changes wrought by such programming have positive implications with respect to issues of police liability and reduced law suits. Additionally, they see more harmonious police-community relations as an effective means to reassert the legitimacy and thus the authority of the police in minority communities (Barlow and Barlow, 1993).

It is a daunting task to attempt to synthesize the array of cultural diversity training initiatives. There are nearly as many approaches as there are police departments, each with its own set of assumptions and related content and delivery style. However, perhaps the most concise means of categorizing cultural training is to follow Rowe and Garland's (2003) typology of cognitive, behavioral, and affective/attitudinal approaches. The first has arguably been the most common strategy historically, perhaps because it appears at first blush to be the "simplest." Briefly, cognitive approaches involve the relatively static delivery of "factual" information about the communities in question. They present participants with a catalog of "typical" behaviors, values and mores associated with diverse groups, and some related details on how to "communicate" effectively in light of those factors.

Such a delivery method obviously has serious limitations. As noted, it is static, implying that particular groups are a) unchanging, and b) monolithic. In so doing, cognitively based curricula often have the counterproductive effect of reinforcing rather than challenging damaging stereotypes (Blakemore, Barlow and Padgett, 1995). So, for example, to highlight the problem of substance abuse within Native American communities reinforces the "drunken Indian" stereotype, without unpacking the structural conditions that have given rise to this problem.

As an alternative, affective programming encourages officers to develop anti-racist (or anti-homophobic or anti-xenophobic, etc.) values and attitudes. In short, these approaches seek to create "reflective practitioners" who are "able to recognize the impact that they personally, and the police service in general, have on the broader community" (Rowe and Garland, 2003: 408). Consequently, officers are challenged to recognize and confront their own racism and its effect on their treatment of and relationship with community members. Typically, this is accomplished by one of two methods, sometimes in concert: first-hand accounts presented by community members; and/or academic accounts of those encounters and their effects.

Two key limitations are generally associated with this approach. First, of the three strategies, it is the most likely to generate resistance and hostility on the part of police officers. They feel that they are labeled as racist, that all blame for the uneasy relationship is placed squarely at their feet, rather than shared with the community. A trainer cited by Rowe and Garland (2003: 406) observed that

> because we're talking about people's values, we're talking about what makes them a person, and we're asking people to look at themselves, reflect on themselves. . . . It's quite an uncomfortable process for these people. When something's uncomfortable for you, then it's a natural reaction sometimes to be hostile.

Officers often see affective programs as a direct threat to their sense of self. They feel that they are being attacked at the very immediate level of who they are and how they think. Consequently, they resist the programming and its messages (Gould 1997).

The second limitation of affective curricula is that they don't typically manifest in long term behavioral change. An evaluation of an affective paradigm conducted by Rowe and Garland (2003) found that participants had difficulty in translating their training experience to the workplace. In particular, they were unable to identify concrete ways in which their workplace behavior differed as a result of what they learned.

Finally are the cultural awareness programs that are expressly intended to affect behavioral change, regardless of what changes may or may not occur with respect to prejudicial attitudes. Such initiatives educate police officers on "appropriate" and "culturally sensitive" ways to deal with minority communities. In short, traditional methods of police training about techniques and procedures are simply translated into how to interact with minority communities. Foremost among the techniques are cross-cultural communication and conflict resolution (Blakemore, Barlow, and Padgett, 1995). Officers' comments in response to one such training initiative reveal the extent to which this sort of approach is exploited by officers who are "looking for guidance on how to manipulate specific groups of people more effectively." One officer specifically asked how he could stop a vehicle driven or occupied by black people, which for him was "suspicious" in his territory. So, for this officer and many others, cultural awareness training was not meant to enhance police-community relations, but to mask the racism that informs their daily practices.

The problem with the latter approach, indeed with all three approaches, is that they share the common and fatal flaw of individualizing the problems of racism and discrimination. Few cultural awareness curricula ask officers and staff to look beyond their individual biases to the cultural contexts that support them. For example, they don't trace the history of the use of police as an oppressive force at the forefront of the processes of colonization. As I have argued throughout this book, the role of law enforcement is not to challenge the power relations that continue to subordinate Native Americans, but rather to reinforce them. It should come as no surprise, then, that diversity training focuses on micro-level rather than systemic problems. This does nothing to challenge either the broad social conditions or the police culture that give rise to existing relations of inequality, which police are bound to defend through the application of coercive power. Indeed, "cultural diversity awareness training cannot change the fact that the basic purpose of policing is to maintain social control by repressing certain activities and restricting freedoms" (Barlow and Barlow, 1993). Moreover, they are charged with policing particular "problem populations"—i.e., poor and racialized communities. Policing represents a racialized drama, played out with the express intent of restricting the movements and activities of racialized groups, including Native Americans.

The "feel good" nature of cultural awareness training—window-dressing as many critics have called it (Rowe and Garland, 2003)—provides legitimacy for coercive, often discriminatory patterns described throughout this book. Like the community policing initiatives of which it is a part, such training masks the racism and inequality it claims to confront, since "questioning institutional power in the perpetuation of racism remain unanswered by an approach that concentrates on the personal traits, norms and mores of staff" (Rowe and Garland, 2003: 408). In sum, cultural awareness training is not an effective means by which to overcome the disparate policing of Native American communities.

Community Policing

As suggested above, one of the reasons that cultural awareness training has had limited impact in minimizing racialized policing is that it has typically been embedded within the broader philosophy, rhetoric and practices associated with community policing. Regardless of the community in question, police reformers since the late 1970s have advocated community policing as a means of not only reducing crime but also enhancing the relationship between police and the people they are meant to serve. Moreover, the same social conditions that gave rise to the impetus for cultural awareness training also gave rise to community policing: public inquiries into police wrongdoing; riots and other large scale reactions against particular cases of police brutality (e.g., Rodney King); and general dissatisfaction and anger toward police on the part of communities of color.

On the face of it, community policing appears to lend itself to anti-racist policing. It is in many respects preferable to the traditional bureaucratic model of policing which is grounded in a hierarchical and adversarial model, very much in conflict with traditional Native American emphasis on healing and restoration: "The concepts of adversarialism, accusation, confrontation, guilt, argument, criticism, and retribution are alien to the Aboriginal value system" (Hamilton and Sinclair, 1991: 37). Moreover, many observers argue that Native American sovereignty and self-government are unattainable without the development of democratic and accountable institutions, as represented by community-based policing models (Luna-Firebaugh, 2007).

Indeed, the philosophy of community policing promises a more democratic and inclusive approach to law enforcement. In contrast to bureaucratic models, it emphasizes community involvement, proactive strategies, and decentralization of control. In theory, such a model engages police and the communities they serve in the collaborative exercise of constructive problem solving. According to an Arizona community policing training manual designed specifically for Indian Country, community policing is grounded in three interconnected principles: community partnerships, problem solving, and supportive organizational change (Inter-tribal Council of Arizona, Inc., 1998). In practice, this can take diverse forms, as the strategies that have developed around community policing are many and varied. Significantly, the identification of problems and their solutions are meant to evolve organically out of the needs, norms and aspirations of the local community. As a small sample, consider the following list of related initiatives: school based crime prevention programs (e.g., DARE); attending Neighborhood Watch and other neighborhood based meetings; collaborating with and learning from community agencies; providing alternative dispute resolution resources; creation of local advocacy boards; civilian law enforcement academies; distribution of police newsletters. Cumulatively, the myriad strategies are intended to break down barriers between police and the public, and to involve the latter in both identifying problems and solutions. Moreover, because the focus is on the local context, it allows for culturally specific approaches. Hence, both the philosophy and practices of community policing seem aptly suited meeting the needs of Native American communities:

> The overarching lesson of community policing is that if reservation police were to pay attention to these problems and were to use credible tribal approaches as remedies, they would become more effective problem solvers, more respected tribal citizens, and better able to "nip in the bud" problems with the potential to escalate into more serious problems (Wakeling, et al., 2001: 55).

In recent years, many law enforcement agencies serving Native American communities have opted for this approach. The Arizona manual mentioned above provides guidelines for implementing the philosophy in Indian Country, and provides brief summaries of the resultant practices on a handful of reservations. The Ak-Chin Police Department, for example, developed a Community Relations Team, tasked with building trust among local youth, in particular. The Cocopah Tribe exploits a Neighborhood Watch program as a means to encourage the public to share information with police. And the Tohono O'Odham Nation Police Department has been very active in building partnerships with local agencies as a means of connecting with the community and identifying its local needs. Wakeling et al. (2001) suggest other very specific changes in policies and procedures as examples of ways of making law enforcement more responsive to local traditions: encouraging local elders to accompany officers responding to calls for service; allowing parties to "talk things out" (as in O'Odham culture) in a supervised setting; and evaluation of officers in accordance with their "fit" with local culture (e.g., Fort Berthold's Black Mouth Society).

Regardless of the community in question, community policing has garnered mixed reviews. Proponents contend, of course, that it has been effective at reducing crime, and fear of crime, and improving relations between police and the public. But detractors question the cost of such successes. Cynically, some contend that reform in the direction of community policing has generally been driven by greed for the lucrative funding available for related programming rather than any genuine concern about "community involvement" (Websdale, 2001; Bolton and Feagin, 2004). Consequently, it is no surprise that the turn to community policing has made limited impact in many cases. Moreover, the philosophy of community policing has often been characterized as a façade behind which law enforcement is able to mask heightened surveillance of "problem" communities.

In a related vein, it has been argued that programs like Neighborhood Watch and others that are grounded in public surveillance often reduce police-citizen "partnerships" to one in which community members become little more than sources of information to police, where they come to be seen by officers "not as co-equal partners, but as junior deputies in police-sponsored crime control efforts" (Beckett and Sasson, 2000: 208). This appears to be confirmed by Neugebauer's (1999) interviews with Canadian Aboriginal people. Participants were skeptical about the sincerity of community policing initiatives, which were seen as efforts to extend police control through information gathering, rather than to democratize their role. Respondents felt that "communication with the police was neither open nor reciprocal. Such efforts to improve police-community relations were very superficial, an exercise in impression management based on self-serving police priorities" (Neugebauer, 1999: 261). In sum, community members—especially those with lengthy histories of disparate policing—recognize that community policing practice rarely coincides with philosophy. Rather, it has the potential to reinforce the distrust of police instead of allaying it (Gabbidon and Taylor Green, 2005; Skogan, DuBois, Gadell, and Fagan, 2002).

Exacerbating this trend is the fact that, ironically, community policing is often aligned with other seemingly contradictory contemporary policing trends. Without obvious awareness of their incongruity, police departments have simultaneously embarked on the move toward community policing and "zero tolerance" or "broken windows" approaches. According to the latter model, harsh and immediate police attention to signs of community disorder is the most effective crime prevention strategy.

In the sort of "us" vs. "them" punitive climate engendered by zero tolerance policing, community policing initiatives are doomed to failure, if only because they further alienate the minority populations that are often the target of both. Here problem identification and problem solving often disproportionately point to minority communities as inherently criminal and in need of heightened police activity. In cities like New York City, where zero tolerance policing really took hold in the 1990s, African Americans and Latinos were disproportionately the subjects of police activities like stops and arrests. Moreover, complaints against police by people of color have also increased dramatically in such cities (Beckett and Sasson, 2000; Bass, 2001). As Beckett and Sasson (2000: 209) conclude, "despite all the talk about community policing, policing practices have become more aggressive and often keep the community in a very passive position *vis à vis* the police."

Finally, with respect to Native American communities specifically, community policing poses problems because it remains predicated on an order maintenance approach that is itself embedded in a Western legal order. It does not constitute a distinct and autonomous system of justice, but rather replicates conventional Western models. As such, it remains a tactic of cultural imperialism and control. Consequently, community policing can be "accused of merely reinforcing the same old (White) laws in a new way. . . . Some will see community policing as a system tied too closely to the establishment and hence reject it" (Skoog, 1996: 127). As suggested above, experiences in many minority communities testify to the counterproductive impact of community policing, which has facilitated enhanced surveillance of communities of color. Rather than contribute to the emergence of anti-racist practices, it has exacerbated the tendency to over-police minority communities. It leaves unchanged the uneasy relationship between the police and the policed.

(E)Race-ing Law Enforcement: Recruiting Native Officers

Optimistically, police reformers in recent years assumed that the inclusion of officers from communities of color would ensure the success of not just community policing, but policing generally. In Indian Country, this practice predates the 1965 Law Enforcement Assistance Act that jump-started the hiring of more minority officers. As chapter 3 revealed, Indian scouts or officers were very early recognized as vital elements in the control of Native American communities. However, the practice has become even more common in recent years.

The emerging literature on the presence and impact of racism against non-white police officers in the Western nations like the United States, the United Kingdom, and Canada is consistent and convincing. Recent studies of both former and serving officers show the extent to which officers perceived racist behaviour and policies as a normative part of their careers. In the United Kingdom, Holdaway's (2004: 856) succinct summary of the collective findings of research spanning the 1980s and 1990s indicates that such experiences spanned the spectrum from individual acts of racism, to the systemic patterns associated with institutional racism:

> Ethnic-minority officers' experience was of frequent prejudice and discrimination, expressed through joking, banter, exclusion from full membership of their work team, little confidence in the willingness or ability of immediate and more senior supervisors to deal with the difficulties they faced, and an acceptance of the virtual inevitability of racism in the police workforce.

Consistently, Holdaway's respondents, and those queried in other similar studies found that officers from minority ethnic communities felt that they were seen first as black, or Asian, and then as police officers—their racial status could never quite allow them to fully integrate into their professional status; they were prohibited by virtue of their race from joining the "brotherhood." Daily reminders in the form of racial "jokes" and epithets combined with the more subtle forms of exclusion to render them perpetual outsiders (Holdaway, 1996; Holdaway and Barron, 1997). Bolton and Feagin's (2003) interviews with black police officers in the United States revealed parallel findings.

What is more disturbing is current literature which shows the persistence of a discriminatory culture even in light of concerted efforts to confront and reduce racism—initiatives such as those noted in earlier sections of this chapter. Not surprisingly, officers from communities of color are quite skeptical of the depth of the change in police culture. While acknowledging a reduced incidence of blatant and overt racism, minority officers nonetheless experience myriad other forms of exclusionary, isolating, and discomfiting forms of discriminatory behavior. In short, while the talk had changed, the walk had not. The changes appear to have been merely cosmetic, and not to have taken root in the structural or cultural framework within which officers work (Cashmore, 2002).

An important consequence of the above, combined with the persistently contentious relationship between police and communities of color, is that men and women of color are dramatically under-represented in policing in most western nations. In the United States, people of color make up a very small and unrepresentative portion of police departments. There are exceptions to this, such as Washington, DC, and Detroit, where black officers constitute a large proportion of sworn officers (Sklansky, 2006). The issue of representation is even more dismal for Native Americans, who are rarely seen within police departments (Luna-Firebaugh, 2007). Even tribal police departments (discussed more fully below) are not entirely constituted by local tribal members, or by Native American officers (Wakeling et al., 2001).

Increased hiring of minority officers was perceived to be a panacea to the problem of policing racialized communities. It was believed by many reformers that this would bridge the divide between officers and the communities they served, and that officers' knowledge of "their" communities would enhance their effectiveness. This has not generally been borne out by experience. Rather, minority officers are often plagued by "double marginality," whereby they are not deemed fully a part of either their racialized community or the world of policing. On the one hand, members of minority groups who choose a career in law enforcement fear being perceived as having betrayed their community. On the other side of the equation of double marginality is, of course, the anticipation of the reaction of white officers to non-white officers. The very realistic fear of racism—both individual and systemic—within the profession is a major prohibiting factor to recruitment (Bolton, 2003; Bolton and Feagin, 2004).

For Native American officers, the difficulty of bridging their cultural and professional communities brings unique struggles. They share the general patterns of double marginality. Gould's (1999; 2002) work with Navajo police officers is especially revealing here. Specifically, they find themselves in the dual positions of being "too Navajo" and "not Navajo enough." However, this positionality also posed additional cultural challenges. His participants highlighted the extremity of the cultural dissonance that they faced as Navajo police officers, wherein they felt they were expected to balance traditional and Western practices that were often irreconcilable. Indeed, one Navajo officer that I interviewed in New Mexico shared her insights into the difficulty in dealing with dead bodies. As a police officer, contact with corpses was an expected part of the job. Yet as a Navajo, it posed difficult spiritual issues that might require healing ceremonies.

As noted in chapter 3, Native American officers are correct to assume negative community perceptions of their roles. In some areas that we visited—especially in the Four Corners area—Native American officers are present and visible in both on and off reservation police departments. Participants recognized this as progress of a sort, suggesting that they, too, assumed that having Native officers would enhance the ability of police to deal with Native Americans. However, they were disappointed to see that Native American officers were no better, and sometimes perceived as worse than their white counterparts. The first observations—from two Navajo men—reflect this ambiguity:

Q But a lot of these cops now, don't we have a lot more cops that are Indian too?
A1 Yes, because of that, because they are hiring more Indian cops within the city of Gallup.
A2 But some of those are pretty hard-ass too.
A1 Yeah, yeah, but it, it the state cops, they, they don't play around with you, they, they'll do the same and discriminate against you and more (Males, New Mexico).

The next two exchanges speak more directly to the perception that Native American police officers are also biased in their treatment of Native American citizens:

We have one, we have a Native American highway patrolman, all he does is give tickets to all the Navajos. No special favors there (Female, Arizona).

A Some, but then the Navajo police are right along with them too, now, with the Navajo police, I think is the fact that, 'Hey, I'm wearing a badge, I'm the law, and you do what you want, and you're just nothing but a Navajo or an Indian.'
Q You get that from the Navajo too?
A Um hmm, we get that from the Navajo. Not only with the border towns, but with the Navajo judicial system also, so, that's what's going on now, and it surprises me, you would think that you would try to support, if you're a Navajo, then you'd think you'd do justice, and you'd provide justice, that everything is all equal, no bias or anything, but it doesn't work that way, the whole system is all messed up (Female, New Mexico).

The limited representation and effectiveness of Native police officers is to be expected given the historical antecedents documented throughout this text. Like community policing, the recruitment of Native officers is made problematic by the perception that this too is little more than window-dressing, or a legitimating device intended to render acceptable the imposition of social control on a sovereign people. Recall that that "the fundamental role of police is to maintain social order, and it is within this function that the use of racial and ethnic minorities as police officers can be best explained" (Barlow, 1994: 159).

Tribal Policing and Peacemaking Law Enforcement

As an alternative to the simple integration of Native officers into non-Native law enforcement many communities have turned to the creation of tribal law enforcement bodies. It is here, suggests Luna-Firebaugh (2007: 58), that the combination of community policing and Native officers might attain some measure of autonomous and accountable policing, since tribal officers are "closer to their communities, they generally reflect the diversity of their communities, and they are in the early stages of development."

Given that the intervention of predominantly white law enforcement bodies was interpreted by many as a threat to tribal sovereignty, it seems almost inevitable that many tribes would opt to create their own police agencies. The imposition of Western systems of law enforcement were thought to impose a similarly Western legal and moral order in conflict with traditional life ways and modes of social control. Moreover, Native American communities were sensitive to the historical patterns of colonial racism embedded in non-Native policing structures. With all of the problems noted in this text, it is clear that neither the American criminal justice system generally, nor American law enforcement specifically have been at all interested in ensuring "justice" for Native Americans. On the contrary, they have been concerned with constraining and containing their ambitions.

In response, many tribes have recently opted for the development of their own tribally funded police agencies. As of 1996, 117 tribes had such bodies; by 2000, the number had grown to 171. The intent of such locally controlled agencies is that they are responsive to the needs of the local Native American government and no other level of government. Rather,

> Tribal communities provide their citizens with police services that are uniquely their own. They employ and train tribal police officers who reflect the goals and visions of the community, who are models for their citizens and who seek to provide the highest quality of police services available (Luna-Firebaugh, 2007: 3).

Few comprehensive examinations of tribal policing have entered the academic literature as yet. The most extensive exception to this trend is Eileen Luna-Firebaugh's (2007) recent text, *Tribal Policing: Asserting Sovereignty, Seeking Justice*. This represents a systematic overview of the philosophies and realities of tribal policing in the United States. She contends that the operation of independent, tribally controlled law enforcement agencies represents a crucial link in the realization of Native sovereignty, to the extent that it is a reflection of tribal rights to shape and enforce their own laws. Specifically, "a tribal police department, if nothing else, serves as a declaration of sovereignty, of the intent of a tribal government to protect and serve its own citizens, and to render justice in a manner understandable to and supported by the community" (Luna-Firebaugh, 2007: 8).

Of special note here is the Navajo Nation Police. Founded in 1936, it remains among the oldest and certainly the largest tribal police department in the United States. Unique to Navajo Nation is the presence of a police training academy responsible for training what are now nearly 300 commissioned officers. Another distinguishing feature of the Navajo Nation justice system in general is the institutionalized existence of Peacemaker Courts, grounded in traditional Navajo methods of "talking things out" among victim, offender, and family/clan members. The goal here is to heal and restore harmony to the community rather than to render any form of punishment.

While antithetical to the traditional crime control model formally practiced by Navajo Nation police, the application of peacemaking principles has been gathering support in recent years. Individual officers have taken it upon themselves to refer matters to local peacemakers. More recently, there has been some movement toward initiatives that train police officers as peacemakers, or ensure that peacemakers accompany tribal officers (Bluehouse, nd). Here would be a case where tribal police truly reflect the values and traditions of their people.

However, more typically, the extent to which existing tribal police departments can further the claim to sovereignty is hampered by myriad cultural and structural barriers. Tribally funded agencies are plagued by the same resource issues as others in Indian Country: under-funding, understaffing, and low pay among them. In fact, these problems are exacerbated by the economic constraints faced by often poor tribes. Hence, the dangers faced by single officers policing wide expanses of land with back-up hours away are enhanced dramatically.

Adding to the problems of tribal police departments is the frequent lack of standard police training. Often, the training offered to tribal officers differs substantially from that offered their POST (Police Officer Standard and Training) trained counterparts. To their credit, tribes make concerted efforts to provide more culturally specific training, stressing

- An emphasis on wisdom and the exercise of discretion in a manner that focused on Indian communities;
- An emphasis on information needed for day-to-day work and a hands-on approach;
- A less stressful environment, resulting from tribal officers being trained together and an emphasis on Indian Country issues;
- Trainers who are Indians themselves and/or who are involved in and knowledgeable about Indian Country (Luna-Firebaugh, 2007: 73).

Most tribes cannot afford to have their officers off-duty long enough to attend federal or state certification programs, or certainly to complete relevant college or university degrees. Moreover, Luna-Firebaugh (2007) observes that few officers finish such programs due in large part to the distance from home, combined with the failure of programs to meet their specific needs.

Thus, much of the training is of the local in-service kind, delivered by local, and occasionally state or federal personnel. The Indian Policing Academy in Artesia, NM is a valuable alternative. However, the sixteen week residential requirement is trying for police departments and for officers away from their homes and families for extended periods. Thus, it is rarely an option for those outside the immediate vicinity.

Several implications follow from this diversity of training. First, it is very uneven across tribal communities. Each has its own requirements and expectations. Owing to financial constraints, some are less able to offer the array and quality of training they would otherwise like to. Also at issue is the question of turnover. Once officers are trained as *tribal* officers, they become very appealing to other, often wealthier non-tribal police bodies that nonetheless serve Indian Country.

Finally is the relationship that such inconsistent and unique training engenders with respect to mainstream police. Luna-Firebaugh (2007) contends that non-tribal officers tend to regard tribally trained police as inferior, not "real cops," and "little more than security guards." This can pose particular problems in situations that require cross-jurisdictional cooperation.

In general, as has been the continuing thread in this chapter, tribal police are in the final analysis still police officers in the conventional Western sense. While there may be tribally defined protocols, these are in addition to rather than instead of U.S. state and federal codes. Tribal policing does not, in the end, amount to an autonomous system of social control The Navajo peacemaking initiatives noted earlier probably come closest to establishing a culturally specific and unique approach to integrated justice in Indian Country. Yet even here, the use of such courts is not universal, and is not always accompanied by similarly sensitive approaches to policing, or even corrections. Hence, most tribal justice systems, and certainly their tribal police departments remain "White adversarial systems run by Natives" (Skoog, 1996: 129), or what Cunneen (2001) refers to as little more than the "indigenization" of western policing practice, by which "the 'problem' of Indigenous people *for* police is dealt with by their incorporation into modified existing structures. The problem of state policing *for* Indigenous people is left unresolved" (Cunneen, 2001: 228).

Sovereign Policing/Policing Sovereign Nations

Alternatively, a truly sovereign justice system would by fully grounded in the philosophies and values of the Native American community in question. Skoog (1996: 128) provides a succinct image of this ideal:

> The European adversarial approach would be replaced with one based on the principles of peacekeeping, community control, and the autonomy of individuals. In all likelihood, the formal charging of individuals would frequently be replaced by mediation between parties. The courts might be radically different than those seen in White communities. They would be less adversarial and would stress conflict resolution and peacemaking. A wide variety of "sentencing" options would be available, and offenders would only be jailed if they were seen to pose a danger to the community.

From beginning—definition of "crime"—to end—response to crime—an autonomous Native American justice system would reflect the vision, philosophies and practices of a sovereign people, and not an imposed set of responses. This is, of course, part of the broader agenda of decolonization, or the assertion of self-determination. The contemporary sovereigntist discourses can be traced to the social activism of the 1960s, during which emerging American Indian movements made the claim for self-determination over assimilation, and by which they intended

> the right to assume control of their own lives independent of federal control, the creation of conditions for a new era in which the Indian future would be determined by Indian acts and Indian decisions, and the assurance that Indian people would not be separated involuntarily from their tribal groups (Johnson, Champagne, and Nagel, 1997: 14).

These guiding principles remain part of the Indian sovereignty movement to this day. Simply stated, Indigenous peoples have the right of self-determination. By virtue of that right, they freely determine their political status and freely pursue their economic, social and cultural development (Article 3, Draft United Nations Declaration on the Rights of Indigenous Peoples). Article 31 goes even further, to articulate the areas in which self-determination should prevail:

> Indigenous peoples, as a specific form of exercising their right to self determination, have the right to autonomy or self-government in matters relating to their internal and local affairs, including culture, religion, education, information, media, health, housing, employment, social welfare, economic activities, land and resource management, environment and entry by non-members, as well as ways and means for financing these autonomous functions.

Native involvement in decisions affecting their economies, cultures and environments, is paramount to fundamentally altering their circumstances. Grass roots organizing and decision making will reflect the daily realities that currently leave them vulnerable to disparities in policing—who better to determine what employment opportunities are needed, or what political structures will facilitate democratization in Indian Country? Self-guided action plans for economic and social development—in keeping with American Indian and not western values—will enable progress that is sensitive to the specific needs of Native American communities. Both the processes and outcomes contribute to the empowerment of Indian people and nations.

This book has presented ample evidence that we are a long way off from recognizing a system of policing that aspires to the autonomy and decolonization of Native Americans. On the contrary, police have been at the front line of efforts to contain and control people attempting to, first retain, then regain their rights, not just to self-determination, but to land, resources, and economic prosperity. Cunneen's (2001: 250) observations in the Australian context have no less resonance in the U.S., or even in Canada:

> It is difficult to talk seriously about government commitment to self-determination when criminal justice administration prioritises essentially

non-Indigenous modes of neocolonial control. There is an official claim to support self-determination (defined as a form of government policy at the state and territory level), but the reality of criminal justice practices is often the opposite. The process of criminalisation, the denial of human rights, marginalisation and incarceration ensure that Aboriginal and Torres Strait Islander people are maintained as a dispossessed minority, rather than a people with legitimate political claims on the nation state.

It has been the central argument of this book that Native Americans have—in historical and contemporary terms—been constrained and disempowered by the parallel trends of over- and under-policing. Together, the associated practices of police have facilitated both the criminalization and the victimization of Native Americans as nations and as individuals. While recent initiatives to "democratize" and "diversify" policing have been presented as steps toward anti-racist practice, the critiques offered in the final chapter underscore the extent to which this remains an unfinished project.

By far the greatest limitation to the effectiveness of tried and tested alternatives has been their consistent failure to seriously alter existing structures and relationships. They have not been able—or even intended—to radically transform the place of Native Americans, so that they are recognized as valuable and sovereign peoples. In short, contemporary justice reforms have done little to nothing by way of promoting either equality or self-determination for racialized communities like Native Americans. They have not challenged the imposition of white western values, rather the "programs, policies, philosophies and values of the dominant society are taken as a given" (Hylton, 2002: 148). Unless and until Native American communities assume the right to implement locally relevant systems of social control, I am left pessimistic about the potential for eliminating the over- and under-policing of Native Americans.

Bibliography

Adelman, M., Erez, E., and Shaloub-Kevorkian, N. (2003). Policing violence against minority women in multicultural societies: "Community" and the politics of exclusion. *Police and Society*, 7, 105-133.

Amnesty International (2004). *Threat and humiliation: Racial profiling, domestic security,and human rights in the United States.* New York: Amnesty International.

Amnesty International (1992). *Human rights violations against the Indigenous Peoples of the Americas.* London: Amnesty International.

Archambeault, W. (2003). The web of steel and the heart of an eagle: The contextual interface of American corrections and Native Americans. *The Prison Journal*, 83(1), 2-25.

Australia. (1992). *Royal Commission on Aboriginal deaths in custody.* Canberra, AUS.

Bachman, R., Alvarez, A., and Perkins, C. (1996). Discriminatory imposition of the law: Does it affect sentencing outcomes for American Indians? In M. Nielsen and R. Silverman (Eds.), *Native Americans, crime, and justice* (pp. 197-208). Boulder, CO: Westview Press.

Barker, M. L. (1998). *Policing in Indian Country.* Guilderland, NY: Harrow and Heston Publishers.

Barlow, D. (1994). Minorities policing minorities as a strategy of social control: A historical analysis of tribal police in the United States. *Criminal Justice History*, 15, 141-163.

Barlow, D., and Barlow, M. (1993). Cultural diversity training in criminal justice: A progressive or conservative reform? *Social Justice,* 20(3-4), 69-84.

Bass, S. (2001). Out of place: Petit apartheid and the police. In D. Milovanovic and K. Russell (Eds.), *Petit apartheid in the U.S. criminal justice system* (pp. 43-53). Durham, NC: Carolina Academic Press.

Bass, S. (2001). Policing space, policing race: Social control imperatives and police discretionary decisions. *Social Justice*, 28(1), 156-177.

Beckett, K., and Sasson, T. (2000). *The politics of injustice: crime and punishment in America.* Thousand Oaks, CA: Pine Forge Press.

Berrill, K., and Herek. G. (1992). Anti-gay violence and victimization in the United States. In G. Herek and K. Berrill (Eds.), *Hate crime: Confronting violence against lesbians and gay men.* (pp. 19-45). Thousand Oaks, CA: Sage.

Bell, J. (forthcoming). Policing and surveillance. In F. Lawrence (Ed.), *Responding to hate crime.* New York: Praeger.

Bell, J. (2002). *Policing hatred.* New York: New York University Press.

Berry, K., and Henderson, M. (2002). Introduction: Envisioning the nexus between geography and ethnic and racial identity. In K. Berry and M. Henderson (Eds.), *Geographical identities of ethnic America: Race, space and place* (pp.1-14). Reno: University of Nevada Press.

Bhattachargee, A. (2002). Private fists and public force: Race, gender, and surveillance. In J. Silliman and A. Bhattachargee (Eds.), *Policing the national body: Race, gender and criminalization* (pp. 1-54). Cambridge, MA: South End Press.

Black, D. (1980). *The manners and customs of the police.* New York: Academic Press.

Blakemore, J. L., Barlow, D., and Padgett, D. L. (1995). From the classroom to the community: Introducing process in police diversity training. *Police Studies,* 18(1), 71-83.

Blaut, J. M. (1993). *The colonizer's model of the world: Geographical diffusionism and eurocentric history.* New York: Oxford Press.

Blee, K. (2004). The geography of racial activism: Defining whiteness at multiple scales. In C. Flint (Ed.), *Spaces of hate: Geographies of discrimination and intolerance in the U.S.A.* (pp. 49-68). New York: Routledge.

Bluehouse, P. (nd). *Peacemaking and peace officer work.* Unpublished manuscript.

Boldt, M. (1993). *Surviving as Indians: The challenge of self-government.* Toronto: University of Toronto Press.

Bolton, K. (2003). Shared perceptions: Black officers discuss continuing barriers in policing. *Policing,* 26(3), 386-400.

Bolton, K., and Feagin, J. (2004). *Black in blue: African American police officers and racism.* New York: Routledge.

Bordewich, F. (1996). Killing the white man's Indian: Reinventing Native Americans at the end of the twentieth century. New York: Doubleday.

Bowling, B. (1998). *Violent racism: Victimization, policing and social context.* Oxford, UK: Clarendon Press.

Bowling, B., and Phillips, C. (2002). *Racism, crime and justice.* Harrow, UK: Longman.

Bracey, D. (2006). Criminalizing culture: An anthropologist looks at Native Americans and the U.S. legal system. In J. I. Ross and L. Gould Eds.), *Native Americans and the criminal justice system* (pp. 35-50). Boulder, CO: Paradigm.

Brunson, R. (2007). "Police don't like black people:" African-American young men's accumulated police experiences. *Criminology and Public Policy,* 6(1), 71-102.

Bubar, R., and Jumper Thurman, P. (2004). Violence against Native women. *Social Justice,* 31(4), 70-86.

Bunch, C. (1995). Transforming human rights from a feminist perspective. In C. Bunch (Ed.), *Women's rights, human rights* (pp. 11-16). New York: Routledge.

Bureau of Justice Statistics. (1999). *American Indians and crime.* Washington, D.C.: U.S. Department of Justice.

Butler, J. (1993). Endangered/endangering: Schematic racism and white paranoia. In R. Gooding-Williams (Ed.), *Reading Rodney King, reading urban uprisings.* New York: Penguin.

Canada, Department of Justice. (1991). *Aboriginal People and justice administration: A discussion paper.* Ottawa: Department of Justice.

Cashmore, E. (2002). Behind the window dressing: Ethnic minority police perspectives on cultural diversity. *Journal of Ethnic and Migration Studies,* 28(2), 327-341.

Christopher, W. (1992). Report of the independent commission on the Los Angeles Police Department. Los Angeles.

Churchill, W. (1997). The bloody wake of Alcatraz: political oppression of the American Indian Movement during the 1970s. In T. Johnson, J. Nagel and D. Champagne (Eds.), *American Indian activism* (pp. 242-284). Chicago: University of Illinois Press.

Churchill, W., and Vander Wall, J. (1990). *Agents of repression.* Boston: South End Press.

Cole, D. (1999). *No equal justice: Race and class in the American criminal justice system.* New York: The New Press.

Committee on Natural Resources. (1994). *The Indian Law Enforcement Reform Act of 1990, law enforcement issues in Indian Country, and recent allegations of police brutality.* Washington, D.C.: U.S. Government Printing Office.

Connell, R. (1987). *Gender and power.* Stanford, CT: Stanford University Press.

Cook-Lynn, E. (2001). *Anti-Indianism in modern America.* Urbana, IL: University of Illinois Press.

Council on American-Islamic Relations. (2005). *Unpatriotic acts—The status of Muslim civil rights in the United States 2004.* Washington, D.C.: CAIR.

Council on American-Islamic Relations. (2004). *Guilt by association—The status of Muslim civil rights in the United States 2003.* Washington, D.C.: CAIR.

Cunneen, C. (2001). *Conflict, politics and crime: Aboriginal communities and the police.* Sydney, AUS: Allen and Unwin.

Deer, S. (2004). Federal Indian law and violent crime: Native women and children at the mercy of the state. *Social Justice,* 31(4), 17-30.

Deloria, V. Jr., and Lytle, C. M. (1983). *American Indians, American justice.* Austin, TX: University of Texas Press.

Executive Committee for Indian Law Enforcement Improvements. (1997). Final report to the Attorney General and the Secretary of the Interior. U.S. Department of Justice. www.usdoj.gov/otj/icredact.htm.

Faery, R. (1999). *Cartographies of desire: Captivity, race and sex in the shaping of an American nation.* Norman, OK: University of Oklahoma Press.

Fagan, J., and Davies, G. (2000). Street stops and broken windows: *Terry,* race, and disorder in New York City. *Fordham Urban Law Journal,* 28, 457-504.

Fishman, L. (1998). The black bogeyman and white self-righteousness. In C. Mann and M. Zatz (Eds.), *Images of color, images of crime* (pp. 109-125). Los Angeles: Roxbury.

Fixico, D. (1993). *The invasion of Indian Country in the twentieth century.* Niwot, CO: University Press of Colorado.

French, L. A. (2005). Law enforcement in Indian Country. *Criminal Justice Studies*, 18(1), 69-80.

Friedlander-Shelby, V. (1989). *Racism on the Flathead Reservation: A correlation of the Confederated Salish and Kootenai Tribes' ability to effectively self-govern*. Center for World Indigenous Studies. www.cwis.org/fwdp/Americas/flathead.txt.

Gabbidon, S., and H. Taylor Green. (2005). *Race and crime*. Thousand Oaks, CA: Sage.

Georges-Abeyie, D. (1990). The myth of a racist criminal justice system? In B. MacLean and D. Milovanovic (Eds.), *Racism, empiricism and criminal justice* (pp. 11-14). Vancouver: Collective Press.

Goldberg C., and Singleton, H. V. (2005). *Public Law 280 and law enforcement in Indian Country-Research priorities*. Washington, D.C.: National Institute of Justice.

Gordon, P. (2000). Black people and the criminal law: Rhetoric and reality. In Robynne Neugebauer (Ed.), *Criminal injustice: Racism in the criminal justice system* (pp. 355-374). Toronto: Canadian Scholar's Press.

Gould, L. (2006). Alcoholism, colonialism, and crime. In J. I. Ross and L. Gould (Eds), *Native Americans and the criminal justice system* (pp. 87-102). Boulder, CO: Paradigm.

Gould, L. (2002). Indigenous People policing Indigenous People: The potential psychological and cultural costs. *The Social Science Journal*, 39, 171-188.

Gould, L. (1999). The impact of working in two worlds and its effect on Navajo police officers. *Journal of Legal Pluralism*, 44, 53-71.

Gould, L. (1997). Can an old dog be taught new tricks? Teaching cultural diversity to police officers. *Policing*, 20(2), 339-352.

Greenfield, L., and Smith, S. (1999). *American Indians and crime*. Washington, D.C.: Bureau of Justice Statistics.

Grenier, L. (1998). *Working with Indigenous knowledge*. Ottawa: International Development Research Centre.

Guerrero, M. (1992). American Indian water rights: The blood of life in Native North America. In A. Jaimes (Ed.), *The state of Native America* (pp. 189-216). Boston: South End Press.

Guyette, S. (1983). *Community based research: A handbook for Native Americans*. Los Angeles: American Indian Studies Center.

Hagan, F. (1993). *Research methods in criminal justice and criminology*. New York: MacMillan.

Hall, S., Critcher, C., Jefferson, T., Clarke, T., and Roberts, B. (1978). *Policing the crisis*. London: MacMillan

Hamilton, A. C., and Sinclair, C. M. (1991). *The justice system and Aboriginal People: Report of the Aboriginal justice inquiry of Manitoba*. Winnipeg: Queen's Printer.

Harding, J. (2000). Policing and Aboriginal justice. In R. Neugebauer (Ed.), *Criminal injustice: Racism in the criminal justice system* (pp. 209-230). Toronto: Canadian Scholar's Press.

Harring, S. (1994). *Crow Dog's case: American Indian sovereignty, tribal law, and United States law in the nineteenth century*. Cambridge, MA: Cambridge University Press.

Harris, D. (1999). The stories, the statistics, and the law: Why driving while black matters. *Minnesota Law Review*, 84(2), 265-326.

Her Majesty's Inspectorate of Constabulary. (1997). *Winning the race: Policing plural communities*. London: Home Office.

Holdaway, S. (2004). The Development of Black Police Associations: Changing articulations of race within the police. *British Journal of Criminology*, 44, 854-865.

Holdaway, S. (1996). *The racialisation of British policing*. Basingstoke, UK: Macmillan.

Holdaway, S., and Barron, A. M. (1997). *Resigners? The experience of black and Asian police officers*. Basingstoke, UK: Macmillan.

Home Office. (2004). *Race and the criminal justice system: An overview of the complete statistics 2002-2003*. London: Home Office.

Home Office. (2000). *Statistics on race and the criminal justice system 2000*. London: Home Office.

Hurtado, A. (1997). When strangers met: Sex and gender on three frontiers. In E. Jameson and S. Armitage (Eds.), *Writing the range: Race, class, and culture in the women's west* (pp. 97-142). Norman, OK: University of Oklahoma Press.

Hylton, J. (2002). The justice system and Canada's Aboriginal Peoples: The persistence of racial discrimination. In W. Chan and K. Mirchandani (Eds.), *Crimes of colour: Racialization and the criminal justice system in Canada* (pp. 139-156). Peterborough, ON: Broadview Press.

Institute for Natural Progress. (1992). In usual and accustomed places: Contemporary American Indian fishing rights struggles. In A. Jaimes (Ed.), *The state of Native America* (pp. 217-240). Boston: South End Press.

Inter Tribal Council of Arizona, Inc. (1998). *Community oriented policing: The American Indian perspective*. Phoenix: Inter Tribal Council of Arizona, Inc.

Jefferson, T. (1994). Discrimination, disadvantage and police work. In D. Baker (Ed.), *Reading racism and the criminal justice system* (pp. 243-258). Toronto: Canadian Scholars' Press.

Jimson, T. (1992). *Reflections on race and manifest destiny*. Center for World Indigenous Studies. www.cwis.org/fwdp/Americas/manifest.txt.

Johnson, B., and Maestas, R. (1979). *Wasi-chu: The continuing Indian wars*. New York: Monthly Review Press.

Johnson, T., Champagne, D., and Nagel, J. (1997). American Indian activism and transformation: Lessons from Alcatraz. In T. Johnson, D. Champagne, and J. Nagel (Eds.). *American Indian activism* (pp. 9-44). Urbana, IL: University of Illinois Press.

Kennedy, R. (1997). *Race, crime and the law*. New York: Vintage Books.

Kerner, O. (1968). *Report of the National Advisory Commission on Civil Disorders*. Washington, D.C.: U.S. Government Printing Office.

Knepper, P., and Puckett, M. (1995). The historicity of Hillerman's Indian Police. *Journal of the West*, 33, 13-18.

LaPrairie, C. (1994). *Seen but not heard: Native People in the Inner City*. Ottawa: Department of Justice.

Leadership Conference on Civil Rights. (2002). *Justice on trial: Racial disparities in the American criminal justice system*. Washington: LCCR.

Levin, B. (1999). Hate Crimes: Worse by Definition. *Journal of Contemporary Criminal Justice*, 15, 1-21.

Luna, E. (1998). The growth and development of tribal police: Challenges and issues for tribal sovereignty. *Journal of Contemporary Criminal Justice*, 14(1), 75-86.

Luna-Firebaugh, E. (2007). *Tribal policing: Asserting sovereignty, seeking justice*. Tucson: University of Arizona Press.

Luna-Firebaugh, E., and Walker, S. (2006). Law enforcement and the American Indian: challenges and obstacles to effective law enforcement. In J. I. Ross and L. Gould (Eds.), *Native Americans and the criminal justice system* (pp. 117-134). Boulder, CO: Paradigm Publishers.

MacPherson, W. (1999). *Stephen Lawrence Inquiry*. London: HMSO.

Manitoba. (1991). *Public inquiry into the administration of Aboriginal justice and Aboriginal Peoples: Report of the Aboriginal Justice Inquiry of Manitoba: The justice system and Aboriginal Peoples, Vol. 1*. Winnipeg: Queen's Printer.

Mann, C. (1993). *Unequal justice*. Bloomington, IN: Indiana University Press.

McGillivray, A., and Comaskey, B. (1999). *Black eyes all of the time: Intimate violence, Aboriginal women, and the justice system*. Toronto: University of Toronto Press.

Melton, A. (1998). Images of crime and punishment: Traditional and contemporary tribal justice. In C. Mann and M. Zatz (Eds.), *Images of color, images of crime* (pp. 58-71). Los Angeles: Roxbury.

Messerschmidt, J. (1983). *The trial of Leonard Peltier*. Boston: South End Press.

Miller, J. (1996). *Search and destroy*. New York: Cambridge University Press.

Million, D. (2000). Policing the Rez: Keeping no peace in Indian Country. *Social Justice*, 27(3), 101-119.

Mirchandi, K., and Chan, W. (2002). From race and crime to racialization and criminalization. In W. Chan and K. Mirchandi (Eds.), *Crimes of colour: Racialization and the criminal justice system in Canada* (pp. 9-22). Toronto: Broadview Press.

Mollen, M. (1994). *The City of New York Commission to Investigate Allegations of Police Corruption and the Anti-Corruption Procedures of the Police Department*. New York.

Myrdal, G. 1984 [1944]. *An American dilemma*. New York: McGraw-Hill.

Nagel, J. (2003). *Race, ethnicity, and sexuality: Intimate intersections, forbidden frontiers*. New York: Oxford University Press.

Nenadic, N. (1996). Femicide: A framework for understanding genocide. In D. Bell and R. Klein (Eds.), *Racially speaking: Feminism reclaimed* (pp. 456-464). North Melbourne, AUS: Spinfex.

Neugebauer, R. (2000). Kids, cops and colour: The social organization of police-minority youth relations. In R. Neugebauer (Ed.), *Criminal injustice: Racism in the criminal justice system* (pp. 83-108). Toronto: Canadian Scholar's Press.

Neugebauer, R. (1999). First Nations People and law enforcement: community perspectives on police response. In M. Corsianos and K. A. Train (Eds.), *Interrogating social justice: Politics, culture and identity* (pp. 247-269). Toronto: Canadian Scholar's Press.

Nielsen, M. (2000). Non-Indigenous scholars doing research in Indigenous justice organizations: Applied issues and strategies. Paper prepared for the Western Social Sciences Association Annual Meeting, San Diego, CA, April 26-29.

Nielsen, M., and Silverman, R. (Eds.) (1996). *Native Americans, crime and justice.* Boulder, CO: Westview.

Nolan, J., Bennett, S., and Goldenberg. P. (forthcoming). Hate crime investigations. In F. Lawrence (ed.), *Responding to hate crime.* New York: Praeger.

Novick, M.. (1995). *White lies, white power.* Monroe, ME: Common Courage Press.

Omi, M., and Winant, H. (1994). *Racial formation in the United States*, 2nd ed. New York: Routledge.

Ontario Human Rights Commission. (2003). *Paying the price: The human cost of racial profiling.* Toronto: Ontario Human Rights Commission.

Ortiz, R. (1981). Foreword. In J. Forbes (Ed.), *Native Americans and Nixon: Presidential politics and minority self determination* (pp. i-iv). Los Angeles: American Indian Studies Center.

Osborne, S. (1995). The voice of the law: John Marshall and Indian land rights. In M. Green (Ed.), *Issues in Native American Cultural Identity* (pp. 57-74). New York: P. Lang.

Parker, E. S. (1869). *Annual Report to the Commissioner of Indian Affairs.* Washington, D.C.: Bureau of Indian Affairs.

Parker, R. (forthcoming). Police Training. In F. Lawrence (ed.), *Responding to hate crime.* New York: Praeger.

Peak, K. (1989). Criminal justice, law, and policy in Indian Country: A historical perspective. *Journal of Criminal Justice*, 17, 393-407.

Perry, B. (forthcoming). *The forgotten victims: Hate crime against Native Americans.* Tucson: University of Arizona Press.

Perry, B. (2006). Normative violence: everyday racism in the lives of Native Americans. In A. Aguirre and D. Baker (Eds.), *Structured inequality in the United States: Discussions on the continuing significance of race, ethnicity, and gender*, 2nd ed. (pp. 239-264). New York: Prentice-Hall.

Perry, B. (2006). "Nobody trusts them!" Under- and over-policing Native American communities. *Critical Criminology*, 14, 411-444.

Perry, B. (2002). Native American victims of campus ethnoviolence. *Journal of American Indian Education*, 41(1), 35-55.

Perry, B. (2001). *In the name of hate: Understanding hate crime.* New York: Routledge.

Perry, S. (2004). *American Indians and crime.* Washington, D.C.: Bureau of Justice Statistics.

Poupart, L. (2002). Crime and justice in American Indian communities. *Social Justice*, 29(1-2), 144-159.

President's Commission on Law Enforcement (1967). *The challenge of crime in a free society.* Washington, D.C.: U.S. Government Printing Office.

Razack, S. (2005). Introduction: When race becomes place. In S. Razack (Ed.), *Race, space, and the law: Unmapping a white settler society* (pp. 1-20). Toronto: Between the Lines.

Riding In, J. (2002). Images of American Indians: American Indians in popular culture: A Pawnee's experiences and views. In C. Mann and M. Zatz (Eds.), *Images of color, images of crime*, 2nd ed. (pp. 14-27). Los Angeles: Roxbury.

Rittner, C. (2002). Using rape as a weapon of genocide. In C. Rittner, J. Roth, and J. Smith (Eds.), *Will genocide ever end?* (pp. 91-98). St. Paul, MN: Paragon House.

Ross, J. I., and L. Gould (Eds.). (2006). *Native Americans and the criminal justice system*. Boulder, CO: Paradigm.

Rowe, M. (2004). *Policing, race and racism*. Devon, UK: Willan.

Rowe, M., and J. Garland. (2003). "Have you been diversified yet?" Developments in police community and race relations training in England and Wales. *Policing and Society*, 13(4), 399-411.

Royal Commission on Aboriginal Peoples (1996). *Bridging the cultural divide: A report on Aboriginal People and criminal justice*. Ottawa: Royal Commission on Aboriginal People.

Russell-Brown, K. (2004). *Underground codes*. New York: New York University Press.

Sklansky, D. A. (2006). Not your father's police department: Making sense of the new demographics of law enforcement. *Criminology*, 96(3), 1209-1243.

Skogan, W., Steiner, L., DuBois, J., Gadell, J., and Fagan, A. (2002). *Community policing and the "new immigrants:" Latinos in Chicago*. Washington, D.C.: U.S. Department of Justice.

Skoog, D. (1996). Taking control: Native self-government and Native policing. In M. Nielsen and R. Silverman (Eds.), *Native Americans, crime and justice* (pp.118-131). Boulder, CO: Westview.

Smith, A. (2005). *Conquest: Sexual violence and American Indian genocide*. Boston: South Side Press.

Smith, A. (2003). Soul wound: The legacy of Native American schools. *Amnesty Magazine*, Summer, 14-16. http://www.libarts.ucok.edu/history/faculty/roberson/course/1493/readings/Native%20American %20Schools

Smith, K. (2003). *Predatory lending in Native American communities*. Fredericksburg, VA: First Nations Development Institute.

Smith, S. (1989). *The politics of 'race' and residence: Citizenship, segregation, and white supremacy in Britain*. Cambridge, UK: Polity Press.

Snyder-Joy, Z. (1996). Self-determination and American Indian justice: Tribal versus federal jurisdiction on Indian lands. In M. Nielsen and R. Silverman (Eds.), *Native Americans, crime and justice* (pp. 38-45). Boulder, CO: Westview.

Stannard, D. (1992). *American holocaust*. New York: Oxford.

Stiffarm, L., and P. Lane (1992). The demography of Native North America. In A. Jaimes (Ed.), *The state of Native America* (pp. 23-54). Boston: South End Press.

Subcommittee on Civil and Constitutional Rights (1988). *Anti-Indian violence*. Washington, D.C.: U.S. Government Printing Office.

Subcommittee on Native American Affairs (1994). *Law enforcement issues in the Bureau of Indian Affairs*. Washington, D.C.: U.S. Government Printing Office.

Sumartojo, R. (2004). Contesting place: Anti-gay and -lesbian hate crime in Columbus, Ohio. In C. Flint (Ed.), *Spaces of hate: Geographies of discrimination and intolerance in the U.S.A.* (pp. 87-108). New York: Routledge.

Takaki, R. (1993). *A Different mirror*. Boston: Little, Brown and Co.

Taylor Greene, H. (2003). Do African Americans police make a difference? In M. Free (Ed.), *Racial issues in criminal justice: The case of African Americans* (pp. 207-220). Westport, CT: Praeger.

Teller, H. (1883). *Annual report of the Interior*, House Executive Document No. 1, 48th Congress, 1st Session, Serial 2190.

Uggen, C., and Manza, J. (2002). Democratic contraction? Political consequences of felon disenfranchisement in the United States. *American Sociological Review*, 67, 777-803.

United States Department of Justice (1997). Report of the Executive Committee for Indian Country Law Enforcement Improvements. Washington, D.C.: U.S. Department of Justice.

van Dijk, T. (1995). Elite discourse and the reproduction of racism. In R. Whillock and D. Slayden (Eds.), *Hate speech* (pp. 1-27). Thousand Oaks, CA: Sage.

Wakeling, S, Jorgensen, M., Michaelson, S., and Begay, M. (2001). *Policing on American Indian reservations*. Washington, D.C.: National Institute of Justice.

Washburn, W. (1971). *Red man's land/White man's law*, 2nd ed. Norman, OK: University of Oklahoma Press.

Websdale, N. (2001). *Policing the poor: From slave plantation to public housing*. Boston: Northeastern University Press.

West, C., and Fenstermaker, S. (1993). Power, inequality and the accomplishment of gender: An ethnomethodological view. In P. England (Ed.), *Theory on gender. Feminism on theory* (pp. 151-174). Hawthorne, NY: Aldine de Gruyter.

West, C. (1994). *Race matters*. New York: Vintage.

Whaley, R., and Bressette, W. (1994). *Walleye Warriors: An effective alliance against racism and for the earth*. Philadelphia: New Society Publishers.

Whitfield, J. (2004). *Unhappy dialogue: The Metropolitan Police and black Londoners in post-war Britain*. Devon, UK: Willan.

Wickersham Commission (1931). *Report on lawlessness in law enforcement*. Washington, D.C.: U.S. Government Printing Office.

Williams, H., and Murphy, P. (1990). *The evolving strategy of police*. Washington, D.C.: National Institute of Justice.

Williams, R. A. Jr. (1990). *The American Indian in western legal thought: The discourses of conquest*. New York: Oxford University Press.

Winant, H. (1997). Where culture meets structure. In D. Kendall (Ed.), *Race, class and gender in a diverse society* (pp. 27-38). Boston: Allyn and Bacon..

Young, I. M. (1990). *Justice and the politics of difference*. Princeton, NJ: Princeton University Press.

Young, M. (1996). Conflict resolution on the Indian frontier. *Journal of the Early Republic*, 16, 1-19.

Index

American Indian movement, 16, 103

Black, Donald, 15, 21, 28, 61
borders, 53-54, 86-88, policing of, 21, 54, 87-88
bordertowns, 6, 9, 84
boundaries (see borders)
Bureau of Indian Affairs, 36, 37, 38, 40, 41, 44, 45, 62

Canadian Inquiry into the Administration of Justice and Aboriginal People, 22
"canteen culture, " 19-22
Christopher Commission, 10, 19
colonialism, 2, 3, 4, 10, 35-41, 38, 43, 46
criminal justice system, African Americans in, 2, 13-31, blacks in (see African Americans in), Latinoes in, 2, 15, 17-19, 24, 26, 28
community policing, 12, 18, 91, 93-96, limitations of, 27-28, 95-96, resonance with Native American traditions, 94-95
cultural awareness training, 91-93, limitations of, 92-93
Cunneen, Chris, 2, 3, 29, 37, 40, 61, 72, 73, 102, 103

double marginality, 41, 98-99

genocide, 10, 33-34, 38-39, 40, 50, 73

hate crime, against Native Americans, 1, 6, 8-9, 83, 88, facilitation by police, 9, 70-72, 73-75, 88-90, failure of police to investigate, 29, 64-69, under-reporting of, 29, 68-69

impacts of discrimination, 77-93
Indian Policing Academy, 101

Kerner Commission, 17-18

law enforcement (see police)
Luna-Firebaugh, Eileen, 2, 36, 43, 44, 94, 98, 99-100, 101, 102

Major Crimes Act, 37, 42-43, 45
Manifest Destiny, 10, 33-34
Mollen Commission, 28, 55-56

Navajo Nation Police, 100-101
Native Americans, as police officers, 35-37, 41-42, 97-99, 99-102, assimilation of, 11-12, 33-45, 46, 100, criminalization of, 1, 3-4, 13-14, 30, 41, 46, 54-55, 78-79, 104, disempowerment of, 1, 29, 77, 83-86, 90, distrust of police, 55, 63, 80-83, 97, incarceration of, 3, 78-80, 85, 88, 104, marginalization of, 1, 47, 49, 52-55, 70, 83-86, over-representation in crime statistics, 3, 78-80, research with, 2, 6-8, victimization of, 1, 3-5, 8-9, 88-90

Oliphant, 42, 45, 65
over-policing, 10-11, 22, 22-28, 47-59

Peacemaking, in law enforcement,
    100-101
petit apartheid, 25, 47
police, and the civil rights movement,
    10, 11, 14-16, brutality, 16-18, 20-
    21, 25, 30, 48, 55-59, jurisdictions,
    36-37, 42-46, 61-62, 64-65, 70-71,
    102, minority police recruitment,
    12, 18, 41, 97-99, misconduct, 11,
    17-19, 59-60, 64-72, 74-75,
    negligence, 64-75, relationship with
    White Supremacist organizations,
    30, role in colonialism, 2-3, 10, 33-
    46, subculture of, 19-22, tribal, 35-
    37, 41-42, 99-102
President's Commission on Law
    Enforcement and the
    Administration of Justice, 17
Profiling, 10, 22-28, 47, 52-55, 76-78,
    80, 81, 86-88
Public Law 280, 44-45
Public Law 93-638, 44-45

racialization, 13-14, and
    criminalization, 13, 14, of Native
    Americans, 33-34, of space, 52-55
racism, 1-3, 8-19, 33-34, 51-52, 82, 92-
    93, 97-98, institutionalized, 19-22,
    95, 97-99, 100

segregation, 11, 53-54, 76, 80, 83, 86-
    88
selective enforcement, 21, 22-28, 54
selective protection, 28-31
social Darwinism, 33-34
sovereignty, 10, 33-39, 42-46, 94, 99,
    100, 102-104
Stephen Lawrence Inquiry, 19
stereotypes, 11, 13-14, 19-20, 22, 23,
    33, impact on policing, 19-20, 22,

23, 49-52, 62-64, 68-69, of Native
    Americans, 33-34, 48, 49-52, 62-
    64, 68-69

terra nullus, 34

under-policing, 1, 11, 21-22, 28-31,
    61-75
violence, against Native Americans, 8-
    9, 11, 64-65, 70-72, 86, 88-90,
    against women, 28-30, 72-74, use
    of by police, 15-16, 20-21, 27-28,
    55-59, 82, 84

Wickersham Commission, 17

About the Author

Barbara Perry is Professor and Associate Dean of Criminology, Justice and Policy Studies at the University of Ontario Institute of Technology, and Visiting Professor at Nottingham Trent University in the UK. She has written extensively in the area of hate crime, including several books on the topic, among them *In the Name of Hate: Understanding Hate Crime*; and *The Silent Victims: Native American Victims of Hate Crime*. She is also General Editor of a five volume set on hate crime (Praeger), and editor of *Volume 3: Victims of Hate Crime* of that set. Dr. Perry continues to work in the area of hate crime, and has begun to make contributions to the limited scholarship on hate crime in Canada. Most recently, she has contributed to a scholarly understanding of the community impacts of hate crime, anti-Muslim violence, and hate crime against Aboriginal people.

Breinigsville, PA USA
19 January 2010
230680BV00003BA/1/P